THE SOUND, SENSE, AND PERFORMANCE OF LITERATURE

PN
4145
G43

Don Geiger   University of California

Scott, Foresman and Company
Chicago   Atlanta   Dallas   Palo Alto   Fair Lawn, N.J.

808/5
6275s

Portions of this book derive from
Oral Interpretation and Literary Study, published in 1958,
and from articles that appeared originally in
*College English, Poetry, The Quarterly Journal of Speech,
Speech Monographs, The Speech Teacher,
The Southern Speech Journal,* and *Western Speech.*

PREFACE

To make this book I have severely edited and added considerably to a little monograph, *Oral Interpretation and Literary Study*, published some years ago and now out of print. But the central proposition of that book remains the primary thesis of this one: that oral interpretation or public reading "presumes to be, like other kinds of literary interpretation, a critical illumination publicly offered in behalf of literature."[1] And I continue to refer to a wide diffraction of the light, including the performer as well as his audience.

In the following chapters we shall explore oral interpretation in its relations to literature considered as dramatic discourse. Put broadly, that means that we shall consider literature as discourse conveying the experiences of given persons or "speakers" in given situations. In doing so, we will not be referring so much to some one among competing theories of literature as to, rather, commonplaces of the ordinary reader's, or critic's, experience. As Professors Beardsley, Daniel, and Leggett put it, for example, "what is central to a literary work is always a human situation of some kind," and these authors go on to generalize that "all literary works imply, more or less distinctly, but always to some degree, a speaker."[2] This book, then, represents an attempt to trace out for oral interpretation studies some implications of commonly accepted ways of regarding central aspects of literature.

It would be presumptuous of me to spell out too explicitly the uses of this book in college courses, for the right reader of any volume is he who finds his own uses for it. Doubtless this book's most obvious audience will be found in courses for advanced oral interpretation students. But, like the majority of textbooks used in the beginning oral interpretation course, this one attempts to elucidate principles of analysis of the literary text (see especially Chapters 1-4 and 6) and principles of delivery and performance (see especially Chapters 7-9).

1. Don Geiger, *Oral Interpretation and Literary Study* (South San Francisco: Pieter Van Vloten, 1958), p. 6.
2. Monroe Beardsley, Robert Daniel, and Glenn Leggett, *Theme and Form* (Englewood Cliffs, N.J.: Prentice-Hall, Inc., 1956), pp. xxii-xxiv.

Throughout the chapters are suggestions, usually of an entirely general sort, for various kinds of classroom projects and assignments (see especially Chapters 5-7). Perhaps it is appropriate to report my own experience that the contents herein have been useful in beginning courses in oral interpretation when closely tied to the study of specific literary selections and specific student readings. But used in later courses, with different illustrative and exploratory assignments, the book has also been serviceable. Also, I should like to think that in English departments some teachers of literature and poetry, with a special interest in oral aspects, may find the book useful in this or that context of study.

I will not seem to be sorry for not being more specific about where, at what level, and in what ways this book of principles and analysis of recurrent problems in oral interpretation studies may be used. That depends less on the work itself, I think, than on how fully the instructor who assigns it shares with me an interest in oral interpretation as a means for increasing literary understanding and as a medium of the student's most effective possible expression of achieved critical insight. And much of my enjoyment as a writer briefly laying out his merchandise comes from knowing that the teacher's fun lies not in slavishly following the prescriptions of a textbook but in making the material dance attendance on his own course aims, assignments, and projects.

Let me conclude with a few short remarks to the student, in whatever course in speech or literature this book may find him. Doubtless there is more than one reliable perspective in which we may study oral interpretation of literature. My hope is merely that what follows are among the good perspectives. That means that this is not a book of rules and regulations. Rather, you should think of it as among your means—which should include other writings on oral interpretation and literature, your instructor's lectures and assignments, your class discussions, and above all your own study and oral reading of specific literary texts—for growth in understanding and practice.

Alfred North Whitehead once wrote, "The function of a University is to enable you to shed details in favor of principles. When I speak of principles I am hardly even thinking of verbal formulations. A principle which has thoroughly soaked into you is rather a mental habit than a formal statement. It becomes the way the mind reacts to the appropriate stimulus in the form of illustrative circumstances." Then Professor Whitehead says clinchingly, "Mental cultivation is nothing else than the satisfactory way in which the mind will function when it is poked up into activity."[3] Whitehead's remarks nicely direct our attention to the proper work and responsibility of the oral interpreter of literature. His mind — and body — must "react," alertly, sympathetically, and fully to specific literary texts and to their proper expression and communication. To react, or respond, richly is something that only the reader and interpreter can do: his textbook of ideas and principles cannot do it for him. But perhaps a textbook can help the student and reader "poke up" his mind into right activity. In any event, I should like to offer this book not as a directive from the Colonel, but as a poker. What should I say then? Good poking!

Don Geiger
Berkeley 1963

---

3. Alfred North Whitehead, *The Aims of Education* (New York: New American Library, A Mentor Book, 1949), p. 38.

CONTENTS

CONTENTS

NEW PERSPECTIVES IN

ORAL INTERPRETATION

Since, roughly, the end of World War II there has been a significant shift of emphasis in oral interpretation studies. Not all students and professors of speech approve of it, but perhaps primarily because they are more certain that there has been a change of emphasis than they are of its precise nature. These students are properly skeptical of any development which may seem to threaten sound speech education in any of its aspects, but little in the recent analysis of oral interpretation constitutes such a threat. Rather, current thinking on the subject provides a fresh emphasis on the importance of the special speech act of oral interpretation in literary, and hence in "general" or liberal, education.

True, currently many of us would urge perhaps more strongly than in an earlier day the value of oral interpretation studies to many persons who cannot be, and have no desire to be, expert actors or professional public readers. But it is no threat to the fully effective public reader to encourage, by providing an educational experience in which many persons may share in some measure his own experience in performance, a widening acquaintance with the principles and practice of his art. Provision of such educational opportunity serves rather to illustrate intimately to the student the complexities of that art, and of its actual and potential worth in comprehending, expressing, and communicating literary values.

Let us discuss these matters briefly, as a useful point of departure for our fuller consideration in subsequent chapters of the nature of a literary text and its appropriate reading or performance.

Twenty years ago one could find many a student of oral interpretation, or "expression" as it was still sometimes called, who believed that effective public performance could be expected only from an interpreter who deeply understood literature. Such a student was probably either a conscious disciple of, or was thinking along the same lines as, Professor Samuel Silas Curry who, in the early years of the century, was already laying the ground for proving the fundamental importance of textual understanding to effective public reading. Doubtless it is true that no interpreter, including poor Ion, the rhapsode so mercilessly badgered by bully Plato, has *really* believed that you can brilliantly perform a text whose meaning is lost on you. But there are degrees of conviction in this matter, and probably no one more than Curry has insisted on understanding as central to the interpretive act itself.

To notice this aspect of Curry's work is to notice how awkwardly focused is the view, suggested by some writers, that current oral interpretation theory is "new" in emphasizing the importance of assimilation of the literary text to good performance.[1] But no one could stress that point more emphatically than Curry. In repeating the stress, as they do, more recent writers but make a tradition of his thought in this respect. It was for Curry to emphasize once and for all the importance of understanding the literary text, to performance. What we can say accurately is that recent writers, more than Curry, have stressed the importance of performance to understanding the literary text.

I mean of course that good performance helps an audience to understand the text. But also I mean that the performer's work helps *him* to understand the text—and not good performance only is required in this case, for often enough the rather mediocre interpretation can be insightful to the performer himself, if not always particularly so to his audience or classmates. This stress on the values of performance, and

1. Charlotte Lee reports recent views in *Oral Interpretation* (Boston: Houghton Mifflin Company, 1959), pp. 545-546.

the practicing toward performance, to increasing literary understanding is probably stronger in writings of the last ten to fifteen years than in any previous time, and so the stress may be called "new" if one wants.

We may well suppose that were Dr. Curry alive today he would share our shifting emphasis in oral interpretation studies. His book, *Imagination and Dramatic Instinct,* for example, published in 1896, will seem truly remarkable to the modern interpreter in the importance it places on concepts which have become key terms in recent interpretation theory—to attitude and situation, to point of view and empathic assimilation.[2] True, Curry does not keep a steady eye on the importance of these aspects, or on their organic relations, but that is hardly surprising, for few writers of his day paid much attention at all to such matters. Curry was diligently attending the literary text, but he did so in the perspective of theories of it as emotional expression or thematic illustration.

That is, the student of literary theory at the turn of the century might well have thought of the poem as stimulation to and enrichment of the emotional side of his nature. He might have thought of the poem as Philosophy illustrated and vivified. He might even have thought of it as Religion with a punch. And Curry's writings rather directly reinforce all such views of the poem. But the student at the turn of the century had little encouragement to think of the poem as formed and thus fictive but life-revealing experience. Yet Curry was probably struggling to this view as basic to and explanatory of the others. If so, Curry's erratic and partially conscious, but strong, struggle against the chief critical currents of his time is perhaps best explained by his keen observation of the interpreter's own art, so necessarily based in any age on empathic response to experiential aspects of literature, and to the sharing in—at least during performance—attitudes and points of view within a text.

However it may have been with Professor Curry, it has seemed a natural thing to many students today to join oral

2. Samuel Silas Curry, *Imagination and Dramatic Instinct* (Boston: School of Expression, 1896).

interpretation to the dramatic theories of literature burgeoning in our own time. This union permits us to trace in a single continuous movement, from text through public reader and on to his auditor, organic relations of literature and its understanding to oral interpretation. That is, accepting the literary text, be it play or poem, as essentially a dramatic form of discourse, we stress its experiential relations with the life it represents and the oral interpreter who expresses it.

The modern statement of these relations goes something like this. There is the common experience of life itself, the life that wears you and me out, to our interest, our profit, and our misery. Then there is literature, a representation of some aspect of life, a symbolic modification and interpretation of experience, its actions and its attitudes. And next, for the interpreter, there is his oral interpretation, an expressive action re-embodying and vividly communicating the symbolic experience of the literary text. In "re-embodying" the symbolic experience of the text, the interpreter comes to know something about it, to know it deeply. The essence of the argument at this point is simple. If a piece of literature is a representation of experience, we probably best *understand* it when we have experienced it, and work in oral interpretation holds out the possibility for something of this meaningful experience. Finally, for the auditor, by means of his own witness of and internal participation in the public performance, there is exciting illumination of—indeed, fresh insight into—the formed experience which is the content of the literary text.

Some such outline will suggest the main line of thought about oral interpretation in the last fifteen years. Such a view of the matter helps us put in proper perspective the charge, sometimes made, that recent writers on oral interpretation would minimize the arts of delivery. It is said that the oral interpretation course becomes, under the latest version of the text-oriented dispensation, a course in analysis and so of literary criticism merely. In such a course, it is held, problems of delivery and communication must necessarily be ignored.[3]

3. See Donald Hargis, "Interpretation as Oral Communication," *Central States Speech Journal*, XI (1960), 170-171.

Instead, we would suggest that, in terms of a dramatic stress on the continuity of the interpreter's problems from textual understanding to public utterance, taking time to study the intricacies of a text is not simply a matter of taking that much time away from the study of intricacies of voice and diction or physical gesture. To the student following an experiential or "attitudinal" approach, these matters will not be inviolably separate categories of activity and interest but rather aspects of a continuum of study and application. Ordinarily the student improves most in both textual understanding and expressive action when he works on text and oral interpretation simultaneously.

Still, though a text-oriented dramatic emphasis should not imply lack of attendance to the physical-vocal medium and the communicative process, it does put these matters in a certain perspective, implying an assessment of their importance about which we should be clear. The student will be primarily interested in oral interpretation as a means for improving his relationship to and understanding of literature. He will think of improved delivery as an implicit and instrumental value.

Let me illustrate my meaning. I imagine two different students beginning work in oral interpretation with different expectancies. One of them thinks, "If only I can learn to stop garbling my words, if only I learn to talk a little more like an articulate, intelligent person, I will be glad. And if, by some miracle yet to be wrought by my instructor, I can only stop slouching up to the rostrum and twitching in front of the class, I shall forever bless his good name." Ah, what a humble fellow, and how charming to see himself as his instructor may see him, too! But I imagine also another valuable sort of expectancy, according to which the student thinks, "If only the poem, in its rise and fall in my voice, will claim me, if even for a moment, I am told I will see a new world, or an old world freshly. Well, I'm game to try, and I hope it's worth looking at." Such a student is ready to be possessed by, and so to possess, the literary text. He sets himself to have a little seizure, a seizure of the sort and quality appropriate to the artful drama of the text. Seized, he will be reasonably content.

5

There is no necessary conflict between the interests just cited. The same student may be interested in both slouches and seizures, and the chapters that follow will pay honor to them both. They are parts of a continuum of the interpreter's proper interest and obligation. But if, operating under one sort of limitation or another, the student must choose, let him simply hope that his slouch and his garble will disappear with the text-directed seizure. Let him give to the latter event his first priority in hopefulness, as he feels the poem coming at him like a monstrous angel.

2

ORAL INTERPRETATION

AND LITERARY STUDY

Probably the most noteworthy thing about the title of this chapter to many persons is its improbability. For generations Americans have heard, or have had to hear, pieces read aloud. Doubtless sometimes the experience has been pleasurable, but it has seldom been thought of as a legitimate aspect of literary education.

If some of us now think more seriously about possible relations of oral interpretation to literary study, perhaps the most powerful motivation comes from certain tendencies in modern literary criticism. The nature of this body of criticism, the product of many writers, is too complex a matter to be reduced to one or two effects. Yet, through all its variations, we may see in the modern critical movement a recurring and ceaseless effort to approach ever more closely the individual work of literary art. The brilliant reading, or analysis, of his poem by the "close" or "textual" critic is the trademark of an age.

In the pride of his achievement, however, the modern critic ordinarily exhibits a certain uneasiness. He wants to "deliver up" the work of art in its wholeness to the reader. Yet he recognizes that he must, after all, describe and analyze literary effects, that he must *abstract* from the whole work certain aspects which claim his attention. Consequently, as though he recognizes that his critical cunning may mislead some dazzled reader into thinking the work criticized of secondary importance, the writer warns us that his criticism is not the poem itself and that all paraphrases and critical comments, however perceptive, must inevitably remain *reductions* of the work of art.

If the textual critic cannot deliver up, no matter how closely he may approach, the literary text entire, where shall we find the critic who can?

The answer to that remains the ageless answer: no one but the author can deliver the whole of his text. He cannot do so as critic, explaining what his text means. As critic, even though he stands in a special relation to his text, he is one more person commenting on it, and his comments may well be less valuable than those of other critics. What he can really tell us about his text he has already said, as author. As author, doubtless he can deliver the whole of his text only to that ideal, rather than actual, reader who has no interest in comments *about* a work of art, simply because he so fully comprehends it.

It would be merely silly to think of the oral interpreter as the ideal reader who understands everything. Nor should we think that the oral interpreter can supersede the textual critic, any more than the latter can supersede the historical critic. These critics provide special insights into literature in their own ways. But we may notice that in reproducing effects of the text itself, the oral interpreter approaches the literary work even more closely than the textual critic. In observing that, we thus recognize the likelihood that the oral interpreter is making his own particular kind of contribution to literary understanding.

The kind of contribution he makes overlaps the author's own. The interpreter does not, like other critics, put his insight into the work in words other than the words of the literary piece, but limits himself to the words presented by the author. However, if the interpreter does not merely offer a melodramatic performance but provides his auditor with insight into the work, he sounds the words as once, we may think, the writer himself sounded them in his imagination.

I am thinking abstractly of some nameless author muttering *sotto voce* the poem he has just written, but I am also thinking concretely of Yeats who always "chanted his verse aloud as he wrote, seeking always the right word, which would convey his meaning and yet fit into the sound effect which he desired

8

to create,"[1] and of Melville, buttoning poor Mrs. Melville into a chair after supper to hear him slice off a layer of his latest whale story.[2] It may be said of the unpopular author of *Moby Dick* that he wanted evidence that at least one person approved his work in his own lifetime. Yet perhaps it is as happy for us to think that he was only listening to himself after all, but that he was simply too inhibited a Yankee ever to howl in solitude to the walls.

But in the case of the Irish poet, of whom it has been said that "his poems gain greatly in meaning and dramatic intensity if they are read aloud as the poet intended,"[3] let us have no doubt: he read his work out loud so that he could see what he said, not just the "gist" of it, or the central action, or the structural relations to last week's episode—matters that will permit a student who recognizes them to pass this examination or that—but all of it: the whole trembling, delicate web of relations between this word and that word and the other word, and their relations to the phrasing, and the phrasing's relation to tone, and countless other things that critics probably have not yet got around to labeling. Of course the author, reading his own work, may in part attend his piece as a textual critic might; he may even think, with the historical critic, of this or that element of the literary order as an imaginative projection from the different order of his own life and times. But the author's reading, as author, is more comprehensive than even a combination of critical approaches (if not, with respect to any given aspect, always as thorough). The story or poem which he finally completes—that is, which he recognizes as so much of a formed imaginative world as he is capable of creating—is what he has to say; and we, as readers, are obviously attending best when we read what he had to say in its fullness.

This kind of omnivorous reading is the necessary act of the oral interpreter. We remember that he must sound all the words in their order. He is never at liberty to bundle up

1. Norman Jeffares, "W. B. Yeats and His Methods of Writing Verse," *The Permanence of Yeats,* eds. James Hall and Martin Steinman (New York: P. F. Collier & Son Corporation, 1961), p. 271.
2. Leon Howard, *Herman Melville* (Berkeley: University of California Press, 1951), p. 109.
3. Jeffares, p. 271.

a few lines or pages in a tight—or loose—generalization, but he must tick off the lines and the pages, word by demanding word. Of course the interpreter may cut passages from the pieces he is reading, or provide "bridges" of critical comment between passages. But when he does so, his cuttings and critical bridges must be judged by standards other than those of textual expression—by the standards of criticism, or exegesis, and of public speaking.

Perhaps, rather than referring to Oral Interpretation, we would more accurately think of it as Primary Interpretation of literature, for it is based on a faith that the words in which they are written can explain much of what poems and stories are and mean. Thus, while the textual critic can isolate and describe the "tone" of the poem, the oral interpreter, as primary critic, can give the tone itself, in all its modifications. If close reading can recognize, let us say, the "massive weight of the line," interpretation can reproduce the full, particular effect. If the author's words alone may fully put his images before our inner eye, the interpreter, in sounding them, may nevertheless articulate their emotional correlatives.

Oral interpretation is especially useful, then, in improving the "art of reading." That is, it contributes to an understanding of the qualities and values of specific literary texts. Mastery of specific texts is by no means the whole of literary education. As Professors Austin Warren and René Wellek put it, "To say that literary study serves only the art of reading is to misconceive the ideal of organized knowledge, however indispensable this art may be to the student of literature. Even though 'reading' be used broadly enough to include critical understanding and sensibility, the art of reading is an ideal for purely personal cultivation. As such it is highly desirable, and also serves as a basis of a widely spread literary culture. It cannot, however, replace the conception of 'literary scholarship,' conceived of as a super-personal tradition."[4] Oral interpretation is but an aspect of literary study. There is no question of its being an alternative or a challenge to any other legitimate approach to literary understanding. Clear on the

4. René Wellek and Austin Warren, *Theory of Literature* (New York: Harcourt, Brace & Company, 1956), pp. 7-8..

limits of oral interpretation, we may stand securely within them: oral interpretation is one more means by which the "art of reading," including critical understanding and sensibility, is advanced.

The advance occurs for the auditor. Hearing an efficient oral interpretation, he better understands the literary text in its particularity. But the reader, too, as he works toward full performance, becomes more sensitive to the text. Nor do I mean merely that he must study the text hard if he is to read it aloud adequately. That is, so far as it goes, quite true of course. Most interpreters have long assumed that knowing a text well is the first step toward good performance. But also, working toward good performance is an excellent way of coming to know the text well.

That view, too, rests on the modern (though not uniquely modern) critical emphasis on literature, including poetry, as a dramatic form of discourse. In working toward good performance, the student's attention is vividly directed to the dramatic particularity of the text.

The analysis of literature which is so suggestive of the particular value of oral interpretation as an exploration toward understanding the text is perhaps most simply suggested in Cleanth Brooks's widely circulated view that "the unifying principle of the organization which *is* the poem is an attitude or complex of attitudes."[5] Brooks indicates his understanding of *attitude* quite clearly in many analyses like that of Donne's "The Canonization." According to Brooks, "the poem opens dramatically on a note of exasperation." Soon he finds the speaker of the poem suggesting "contemptuous alternatives," and he analyzes the second and third stanzas of the poem as "modulating from the note of irritation with which the poem opens into the quite different tone with which it closes." Brooks finds further that this third stanza moves from "ironic banter into a defiant but controlled tenderness."[6] That is, the critic finds that the materials of the piece are organized by (or, perhaps more accurately put, he finds that

5. Cleanth Brooks, *The Well Wrought Urn* (New York: Harcourt, Brace & Company, 1947), p. 175.
6. Ibid., pp. 11-20.

the materials or parts of the piece when organized by the poet issue in) an "attitude or complex of attitudes" — like *exasperation, ironic banter, defiant tenderness,* etc.

Brooks's is merely one emphasis of a widely prevalent view of literature as a dramatic form of discourse. Though he is not so insistent as Brooks on the paradoxical and ironical qualities of attitudes in literary texts, R. P. Blackmur suggests that the most successful literature is language that "becomes gesture."[7] Blackmur himself[8] suggests that a counterpart of his own opinion is to be found in Kenneth Burke's view of literature as "symbolic action."[9] Though numerous "new" critics have treated literature as a language of gesture, action, or attitude, the view is not restricted to the new criticism. A "neo-Aristotelian" critic, Elder Olson, though he objects strongly to many aspects of other modern criticism, treats even the lyric poem as the "action or behavior" of "a single character acting in a single closed situation."[10] Or, to take an extreme example, a logical positivist, like Rudolph Carnap, whose analysis of language generally provides little comfort for most contemporary literary critics, suggests a certain affinity with them at this point when he writes of "cries like 'Oh, Oh,' or, on a higher level, lyrical verses."[11]

The oral interpreter is bound to be interested in dramatic analysis of this sort, for it suggests that he is indeed trying to express what the poem *is.* An attitude — like *exasperation,* for example — involves the whole organism. The "mind" records and analyzes the *exasperating* characteristic(s) of some environment, while the "body" reflects in, participates in, and communicates this exasperation in *pursed lips, flashing eyes, clenched fists,* etc. Working toward a performance involving his own organic reactions, the student of oral interpretation must closely grasp the dramatic particularity of the text.

7. R. P. Blackmur, "Language as Gesture," *Accent Anthology,* ed. Kerker Quinn and Charles Shattuck (New York: Harcourt, Brace & Company, 1946), p. 467.
8. Ibid., pp. 467-468.
9. See especially Kenneth Burke, *The Philosophy of Literary Form,* rev. ed. (New York: Vintage Books, Inc., 1957).
10. Elder Olson, "An Outline of Poetic Theory," *Critics and Criticism,* ed. R. S. Crane (Chicago: University of Chicago Press, 1952), p. 560.
11. Quoted by Susanne Langer, *Philosophy in a New Key* (Cambridge: Harvard University Press, 1942), pp. 83-84.

We often hear remarks like George Reynolds', that oral interpretation "can insure that the selection is read in the right spirit—the serious as serious, the humorous as humorous, the ironic as ironic."[12] Once we understand the dramatic nature of literary discourse, we will wish to agree with Professor Reynolds' general statement in detail. We will not attribute qualities like "serious" and "humorous" to whole selections merely. It does not mean much (or rather it does not mean enough, or it may even mean something misleading) to say that *Hamlet* should be read "seriously" or that "The Comedian as the Letter C" should be read "humorously." We should seek instead to communicate those shifts in "spirit"— that is, those continually modulating attitudes—which occur from line to line and even word to word.

Once we recognize the dramatic nature of literary discourse, we must question some generous testimony to the values of oral reading. David Daiches, for example, reports: "I have known students who have been more effectively brought to see the essential life in a poem by hearing it read aloud slowly than by the most careful analysis of its structure."[13] Undoubtedly oral interpretation may have this effect, but it is not really because the piece is read *slowly*. True enough, in the early stages of his study of a poem—in which the "point" is everywhere immanent—the student should usually read slowly. If he does not do it silently, the teacher may well do it for him orally, thus enforcing the act of attention. But, still, opening the mouth and slowly sounding off is not enough ordinarily to bring a piece to its "essential life." This is the result not of reading slowly but of reading well.

What is demanded is, roughly, that the attitudes and actions of the reading be congruent with the attitudes and actions of the piece, and in different pieces these attitudes and actions will develop in vastly different tempos. Clearly, we should not want to hear most of "How They Brought the Good News from Ghent to Aix" read slowly; and when we hear the opening line of "The Canonization," though it may possibly

12. George F. Reynolds, "Oral Interpretation as Graduate Work in English," *College English*, XI (1950), 205.

13. David Daiches, "The New Criticism: Some Qualifications," *College English*, XI (1950), 247.

13

(and probably will not) be read slowly, what we are chiefly interested in having communicated is the proper measure of *exasperation*.

To ask so much from an oral reader is not to ask him to become expert in startling sneers, frightening roars, table-dumping thumping, or the use of mascara. Such wretched and shallow exhibitionism is sometimes wrongly called "acting." Actually, a good job of acting out that which is a "symbolic act" or suggesting the attitudes of that which is a "complex of attitudes" is an entirely legitimate process. But our principal interest should not be in saving the term *acting* even though, as we shall see in a subsequent chapter, the term may be put to good critical use, but in pointing out the difference between effective and ineffective, or even misleading, oral readings.

The reader's choice is not between roaring like a seal and reading aloud slowly and neutrally. In a later chapter I shall discuss at length the relation of oral interpretation to the structure of sounds in a poem. Meantime, we may notice merely that one of the most misleading of all oral readings is a "neutral" one, the reading designed to let the listener "come to his own conclusions." The listener does that anyhow. Actually, by reading "neutrally" that which snarls and smiles (the complex of attitudes lying at the heart of the literary text), the reader probably suggests largely that all literature was written by the same listless author. The only difference in readings by the "neutral" reader is that he reads the "serious" un-seriously and the "comic" un-comically.

The reader's choice is broadly between good roars and bad ones. It is not the roar we should object to; it is the inappropriate roar, and it is a matter of indifference whether or not this unhappy thing is called "acting." A roar that for no good aesthetic reason frightens a listener off his chair has no place in oral reading; a roar that suggests the particular character of Lear's rage may be invaluable.

Students have long recognized this. They remember with keen gratitude teachers who read literature well. Such teachers helped them hear the "very tone" of literature.

Valuable as good reading by teachers may be, it is still

more important for students themselves to read aloud. Work in oral interpretation is valuable because, among other things, preparation for performance requires the closest possible study of the piece itself; because the student's oral readings show him the value of making such analyses; because a public performance encourages responsible, and pleasurable, study; and because his readings carry the student "beyond" analysis.

So far as preparation is concerned, we have said that the oral interpreter may reveal the complex of attitudes which in a significant measure "*is* the poem." But the complex of attitudes is developed only out of the interplay of the piece's separate parts.

In accepting this identification of form and content, the oral reader adopts the generally accepted view that "meter, diction, methods of organizing the poem . . . are . . . parts of the total meaning."[14] In brief, then, the oral interpreter, wanting to convey the attitudes of the poem can only know them when he has traced out the function of diction, meter, images, symbols, alliteration, internal rhymes, etc., or, in the case of prose, plot, description, point of view, character, etc.

The interpreter must, for instance, notice the indifferent rhyme of "up" with "drop" in Yeats's "Leda and the Swan" if he is to suggest fully the *careless indifference* of the god, which is represented in that poem; or he must observe the connotations of "perfume" if he is to convey the *intense irony* of Webster's lines, "All the Flowers of the Spring / Meet to perfume our burying"; or he must notice the length of one of Whitman's lines if he is to suggest the *patient toil* of the spider represented therein; or he must observe the function of the counterpointing of "ambitious" and "honorable" in Antony's funeral oration if he is to communicate all of Antony's *growing irony, sarcasm, hatred;* or he must observe that the imaging of Death as a "slave" in Donne's "Death, Be Not Proud" does much to establish the speaker's triumphant contempt of death. These are merely random samplings of the kind of study an oral interpreter must make and are, furthermore, bold examples of what must be studied in fine detail.

14. William Van O'Connor, "A Short View of the New Criticism," *College English*, XI (1949), 66.

Clearly the student who reads aloud learns the value of such analyses. For example, if the student suggests in his reading a "Mariana" who is slightly tired, he will be reminded that Tennyson has on the contrary—through an almost monotonous repetition of the word "aweary" and the linking of this word by rhyme to "dreary," both of them completing lines in drooping feminine endings—sought to establish her *complete despair,* and that this is an important part of what a good reading of the poem will suggest. Or if, in reading "To His Coy Mistress," the student suggests a speaker who is some politely id-less romantic, he will be asked to brood on the implications of a lover who would give a hundred years of praise to eyes and head, two hundred years to the adoration of each breast, "But thirty thousand to the rest." And, if this leads the student simply to suggest a *leering lover,* still other aspects of the piece will be noted which must qualify this interpretation.

In sum, the attitudes which the reader must convey can only be discovered, and subsequently suggested in a reading, when the parts of the piece from which the attitudes emerge are discovered and understood.

The student who wants to "read out" the attitudes of a piece will be interested in making a close textual analysis so that he can find out what attitudes to communicate.

We have already noted that it is highly appropriate to study the detail of a piece in the dramatic perspective required by performance. Because his analysis ends in a reading, the student is usually motivated to make close analytical studies. He learns why, because he must teach himself why, a poem must be "torn apart." He is less likely to object that all his pleasure has been destroyed by "ripping the poem to shreds." He should learn through his readings that this object in which he takes pleasure is, after all, the configuration of its many parts. A teacher can always *tell* the student this, but the student by oral readings can show and convince himself. It was certainly his realization of this that prompted the French philosopher Bergson to stress the importance of reading aloud for students of literature at all levels of study. Bergson suggests that if the student is to understand and enjoy a literary text he "will first have to reinvent it or, in other words, appropriate to a certain extent the inspiration of the author. To do so he must fall into step with him by adopting his gestures, his attitudes, his gait, by which I mean learning to read the text aloud with proper intonation and inflection." Bergson goes on to say that it is "wrong" to treat reading performance "as an artistic accomplishment. Instead of coming at the end of one's studies, like an ornament, it should be at the beginning and throughout, as a support. Upon it we should place all the rest if we did not yield here again to the illusion that the main thing is to discourse on things and that one knows them sufficiently when one knows how to talk about them."[15]

A further motivation to study is of course that crude but effective pressure of having an audience. Having become, during the time of his reading, the most active agent in the class, the reader does not want to bore classmates who are probably both friendly and critical. He wants to provide as rich an experience for them as he can.

But oral interpretation encourages not only responsible but also pleasurable study, and pleasure of a sort which advances literary understanding for both the student who is reading aloud and his classmates who are listening. Of course we know that we like to share literary, as well as other kinds of, experience. That is why we talk about poems and stories to one another and compare our reactions. In the case of listening with others to a piece of literature, perhaps our appetite for community is merely atavistic, and our pleasure that of huddling together round a flickering fire to hear the shaman chant. Doubtless we prefer to think of the pleasure as humane and civilized, valuable not only in itself but insofar as the text itself becomes more vivid for each member of the community of listeners. We do not know precisely *why* it is that we may respond more fully to a piece simply because we are aware that other persons beside us are responding, too. Furthermore, we recognize that there are times when we want nothing so much as to be alone, and left alone, with a book or a poem. But there is no need to replace one kind of experience

15. Henri Bergson, *The Creative Mind*, trans. Mabelle L. Andison (New York: Philosophical Library, Inc., 1946), pp. 101-102.

17

with another, for there is room for both private and social experience of literature. Here, we are merely noting that frequently a piece of literature may be more vividly realized by a person simply because he is listening to it with other people, the author's good words shining even more brightly in the genial glow of a social occasion.

A further value of oral reading is that the experience it provides both reader and audience takes them, in a sense, "beyond" analysis. I mean nothing mystical but am merely referring once again to the dramatic particularity of the literary text and to the realization that our talk about a piece, even when it is highly critical talk, is not equivalent to the piece itself.

The piece itself, as Burke puts it, is a "new word,"[16] not quite to be captured by any of the words we already have. Blackmur suggests the same thing when he writes of "gesture" that "it is that play of meaningfulness among words which cannot be defined in the formulas in the dictionary, but which is defined in their use together."[17] For example, though it is nearly all we can say *about* it, "The Canonization" does not really begin on a note of "exasperation," not of exasperation-in-the-abstract, at any rate. We know that the "exasperation" of a man who cannot find his shoelaces and the "exasperation" of a condemned man awaiting a tardy governor's pardon are likely to be very different things expressed in widely different ways. So this poem begins with the particular exasperation of a particular man in a particular situation. Brooks takes analysis about as far as it can go in suggesting the quality of that particular exasperation. After remarking that the poem opens on this note, he states the probable characteristics of the person to whom the remarks are addressed: this person represents "the practical world," etc. That is, the critic does what he can to suggest all those special conditions of the attitude which makes this particular exasperation what it is.

Having accomplished this task, talk *about* the matter can hardly accomplish more. What remains is the utterance of

16. Kenneth Burke, "Lexicon Rhetoricae," *Critiques and Essays in Criticism,* 1920-1948, ed. Robert Wooster Stallman (New York: The Ronald Press Company, 1949), p. 95.
17. R. P. Blackmur, "Language as Gesture," *Accent Anthology,* ed. Kerker Quinn and Charles Shattuck (New York: Harcourt, Brace & Company, 1946), pp. 470.

this particular exasperation itself, and this is what the good oral reading can yet achieve.

If work in oral interpretation can increase the student's capacity to understand and enjoy stories and poems, he should give the subject his sympathetic and alert attention. Oral interpretation will not inevitably cause the student to cherish literature. But in its inevitable emphasis on the whole poem it will encourage response. If it will not necessarily make the student understand literature, it will do much to let him understand what his reactions to a piece — which, as we have seen, in his desire to read aloud effectively, he is likely to attend more fully than usual — really are.

Certainly our hope for a wider appreciation of serious literature lies in genuine human response to it. We should approach this topic with guarded gloom. We recognize something merely fashionable in threnodies on the state of letters in society, and it is not a recent fashion either. Ben Jonson, in the Golden Age when serious drama was popular, nevertheless spilled some bitter ink complaining of the poet's fate.[18] Nor is it a recent charge that the better the literary work, the more likely it is to be ill-received. A century ago, Thackeray complained, "One man spends a life of learning and labour on a book which does not pay the printers' bill, and another gets a little fortune by a few light volumes." Nor have literary men, adds Thackeray wryly, "received stars and garters as yet, or peerages and governorships of islands, such as fall to the lot of military officers." Still, Thackeray, cheerfully ready to do without his garters, praised the literary life, and the rich usefulness to man of literature.[19]

Perhaps the amazing thing, in any time, is not that literature is disdained, but that it is honored as much as it is. An appetite for literature derives from certain native sensitivities and verbal talents, and their training. If nothing else, one must contend with so many words. Hart Crane once suggested that a poet must be "soaked in words," and it certainly follows that, if his mind and spirit are to be illuminated, the

18. See J. William Hebel and Hoyt H. Hudson, eds., *Poetry of the English Renaissance,* 1509-1660 (New York: F. S. Crofts & Company, 1929), pp. 901-902.
19. W. M. Thackeray, *Critical Papers in Literature* (New York: The Macmillan Company, 1904), p. 393.

reader must be pretty well splashed in words, too. This does not mean merely that he must be literate. Our modern world is literate, but set adrift in a sea of words it just will not soak. Admitting that a reader of literature must have a sense of words at least equal to the symphony auditor's sense of sound, we should not be surprised to find him of a relatively rare species.

Beyond the difficulty of the literary medium lies the challenge of the complex world it presents. Literature presents the world tentatively, relativistically, and comprehensively: the good man in A's book becomes the bad man in B's, and in C's he is both so good and so bad you do not know what he is; the most significant aspects of life in D's book become hollow mockeries in E's, and in F's book they are simply not worth mentioning.

This is not to suggest that these sometimes contradictory visions, so passionately embraced by their several authors, do not add up to something. On the contrary, they add up to a very great deal; indeed, the virtue of literature's imaginative worlds is to bring us, in their totality, something like the whole of that "real world" (of course this is a reference to the moral world of value even more fully than to the world of physical event) of which, in our private persons, we can directly know so little.

A visitor from Mars would surely be deeply interested in our literature, however lightly he might regard the conclusions of our science and our philosophy; and I suspect that the reader of literature is in something like the condition of a visitor to our planet from outer space — an eager, tolerant visitor, we hope, wishing to know humanity before judging it.

But many of our citizens do not come to us from Mars. They do not care to know how the cannibals live, for they are busy enough frying their own fish; nor do they wish to familiarize themselves with the fauna of Florida, for they live in Utah. "'Books! prithee, don't talk to me about books,' said old Sarah Marlborough. 'The only books I know are men and cards!'"[20]

20. W. M. Thackeray, *The Four Georges* and *The English Humourists of the Eighteenth Century* (London: John Murray, 1869), p. 54.

20

There speaks a good sturdy village spirit and, far from mocking it, the person of literary appetite seeks to attain its security.

I recall having heard of the Catholic sister who, on reading Eliot through "Ash Wednesday," was reported to have said pityingly, "To think of all the poor man had to go through before coming to that." The literary person does not inevitably conclude his tours through the "circumambient gases" of the imagination on Ash Wednesday, but, with luck, he may attain some happy country of the mind, only to discover that someone — Lady Marlborough perhaps — has been there all the time.

Of course we believe that the literary person, writer or reader, though he may be in his fulfillment merely a prodigal son come to some home or another, nevertheless knows better what kind of home it is than all those sons and daughters who have never been away.

But, as it is the fate of the prodigal son to travel if he is to know either himself or his proper home, so is it the fate of the serious reader of books to experience literature, if he is to put at rest that unease of the spirit in which the taste for literature is rooted.

We so familiarly figure the poet in labor, giving birth to his poem, that we are likely to ignore the similar labor of his reader, giving birth to himself. In such births, the reader experiences literature as, in Sydney's phrase, "hart-ravishing knowledge."[21] Oral interpretation, in its emphasis on understanding the dramatic particularity of the text, is one means by which large numbers of students may be led to consent cheerfully to their good hearts' ravishment.

21. Hebel and Hudson, p. 885.

3

EMOTION IN LITERATURE:
THE ORAL INTERPRETER'S
SPECIAL RESPONSIBILITY

We have discussed literature as a dramatic form of discourse. Such a stress implies a high regard for passional aspects of literature—the attitudes, feelings, states of mind, of the "speaker" or speakers within the poem, or story. It may seem an appropriate stress to the "vast majority" of contemporary critics who, according to Eliseo Vivas, conclude that "the artist is primarily concerned with emotion"—that he wishes both to express emotion and to arouse it in his audience.[1] But to Mr. Vivas himself, and to critics like him, who would turn our attention from the emotion which the creative writer expresses, to the objects which he depicts in his piece, our emphasis to this point may seem exclusive and reductive—as though the oral interpreter does not care for the writer's "vision" but only for his fine feelings.

The truth is rather that the oral interpreter must attend to both emotion and object. He attends to emotion, obviously, because he seeks to express it. But he attends to objects, too, and in fact he *must* fully contemplate or "realize" them if he is to express emotion accurately.

To clarify this version of the interpreter's practice, let us turn to a consideration of object-oriented theory. Though we should regard such theory with certain reservations, it has a central soundness which the oral interpreter, for all his

---

1. Eliseo Vivas, "The Objective Correlative of T. S. Eliot," *Critiques and Essays in Criticism,* 1920-1948, ed. Robert Wooster Stallman (New York: The Ronald Press Company, 1949), p. 389.

commitment to passion and emotion, does well to recognize. A recognition of the importance of *things* in poems, and in stories, eventually helps to define and vivify the values of oral interpretation as an approach to literature's *emotion*.

The object-oriented critic's approach has the evident virtue of beginning, generally speaking, where the piece begins. Theories of literature as emotional expression begin instead at one remove, as it were, from the piece. For example, Professors H. J. Hall and J. R. Moore suggest of "the song," considered as a poetic type, that it is "the expression of simple emotion in the most direct and musical form."[2] But when we turn to a typical song in their collection, we see how easily it may yield itself to another order of description:

> When Love with unconfinèd wings
>   Hovers within my gates,
> And my divine Althea brings
>   To whisper at the grates;
> When I lie tangled in her hair
>   And fetter'd to her eye,
> The birds that wanton in the air
>   Know no such liberty.[3]

What is presented to our imagination certainly is a picture of whispering lovers, passionate embraces, prison cells, birds soaring through the air, and a fairly large number of relations—implicit and declared—among these objects.

It is not surprising then that certain critics will give first consideration in their literary theory to these explicitly designated "things." John Crowe Ransom, probably the modern critic best known for an approach to poetry via its represented objects, has stated flatly that poetry gives us "knowledge by images, reporting the fullness or particularity of nature."[4]

This formula, however, may well be too good to be altogether true. We may agree with Mr. Ransom when he suggests

2. Howard Judson Hall and John Robert Moore, *Types of Poetry* (Boston: Ginn & Company, 1931), p. 192.
3. First stanza of "To Althea, from Prison" by Richard Lovelace.
4. John Crowe Ransom, *The World's Body* (New York: Charles Scribner's Sons, 1938), p. 158.

that "the ostensible substance of the poem may be anything at all which words may signify: an ethical situation, a passion, a train of thought, a flower or landscape, a thing."[5] But even if we agree to consider a poem as the representation of an aspect of nature, of the sort that Mr. Ransom suggests, the imaginative construction does not quite seem a "report" of this aspect; certainly it is not a report of its "fullness."

The representative act of the poet is instead probably closer to that which Mr. S. I. Hayakawa attributes to the novelist, who "*abstracts* only the events relevant to his story and then *organizes* them into a meaningful sequence."[6] The poet too "abstracts" or selects from the qualities and objects of his possible subject matter only those which contribute to his purpose. He is, in short, "artist" just because of his ability to select from the fullness of some aspect of nature details which become meaningful in his total organization of them.

Take, for example, two lines from Thomas Hardy's "In Time of 'The Breaking of Nations' ":

Yonder a maid and her wight
Come whispering by[7]

This is the only description in the poem of the two people, and so far as the reported "particulars" of their being together are concerned, the passage is quite bare. All that is actually *reported* is their "whispering." Doubtless what is reported controls our imagination, so that we feel quite sure that they are lovers, and that probably they are strolling along (if they came riding by, the speaker probably could not hear them whispering, though he might). Whether or not they are holding hands, or walking with arms around one another's waists, etc., is not reported, or even certainly implied. Yet the imagination is likely to insist on such a gesture, will conjure at least a fleeting image of their youth, etc.

5. John Crowe Ransom, "Criticism as Pure Speculation," *Essays in Modern Literary Criticism*, ed. Ray B. West, Jr. (New York: Rinehart & Company, Inc., 1952), p. 235.
6. S. I. Hayakawa, *Language in Thought and Action* (New York: Harcourt, Brace & Company, 1949), p. 133.
7. From *Collected Poems of Thomas Hardy* (1923). Reprinted by permission of The Macmillan Company, New York, and The Macmillan Company of Canada Ltd., Toronto.

Nor is the poet's selection of details the only cause of his not reporting an aspect of nature in its fullness. His medium, words, forces on him another sort of abstraction. Literary art, in its densest representations, can hardly challenge even representative painting, much less nature, in particularity. For example, in a poem quite densely thicketed with particulars, Robert Horan's "Little City," there remains a certain inevitable abstraction. Take, for example, the first two lines:

Spider, from his flaming sleep,
staggers out into the window frame[8]

The spider, apparently waking at dawn, is vividly reported as "flaming." But there are all kinds and sizes of spiders, many intensities and possible combinations of color in "flaming," and certainly "window frames" are of many different sorts. The particulars are not really "fully" in the poem, as they might much more nearly be in a painting of the scene, but are filled in by the reader's imagination.

Such an analysis does not mean that poetry should be compared unfavorably with painting. If a painting (of the representative sort) has the advantage in specificity, the poem doubtless has the usual advantage in scope and suggestivity. But the analysis does suggest that formulations like Mr. Ransom's must be importantly qualified in the interest of accuracy.

Yet, however such theories must be qualified, it is also true that they, in turn, serve an important function by themselves qualifying theories of literature as emotional expression.

On superficial inspection, theories of this latter sort would seem to be especially attractive to the oral interpreter of literature. Expression of emotion is thought to be central to his task; certainly the interpreter wishes to "move" his audience. But at least three serious objections are frequently raised against such theories.

First, if a piece of language simply expresses emotion, it need not require "study." According to this objection, we need

8. From *A Beginning* by Robert Horan (New Haven: Yale University Press, 1948).

25

not study emotions (except in psychological ways, as signs of something else); we need only feel them (the implication is apparently that anyone can do *that*). Literary "study," then, must be of other things—of biography, of history, of rhetorical devices, etc.

Second, literature becomes a discourse of secondary importance; if it is "merely" emotive discourse, it is obvious that we cannot gain insight of much importance from it.

Third, insofar as the theory establishes the relation of the oral interpreter to literature, he is likely to be taken for a kind of self-exhibitory, emotional, unintellectual creature, hardly up to the manly task of really *knowing* anything about the piece of literature.

Speculation like Mr. Ransom's, even though we may partially object to it, greatly encourages a defense against such charges. By taking account of the objects and situations which a poem represents, such speculation permits of a quite sophisticated view of the emotion which poetry, as well as fiction, expresses.

Mr. Vivas, for example, stating that he has been chiefly influenced by Ransom, "with his salutary insistence on the ontological interest of the poet," concludes that "the aesthetic of expression is a useless and confusing muddle that mystifies far more than it explains."[9] But this does not mean that Vivas thinks that poetry does not express emotion. Emotion is expressed, but only in a somewhat complex fashion, controlled by and closely related to objects designated by the poem.

In Vivas' own words, "the poem may be about a situation or an object which socially is connected or invariably associated—whether naturally or conventionally—with an emotion." That is to say, "poetry refers denotatively to emotions, not by means of direct verbal reference, but through the whole poem itself."[10]

Mr. Vivas elaborates his view in an analysis of Garcia Lorca's elegy on the death of a bullfighter, *Llanto por Ignacio Sanchez Meljias,* whose opening lines Vivas translates as follows:

9. Vivas, p. 399.
10. Ibid., p. 394.

26

Five o'clock in the afternoon,
It was five sharp in the afternoon.
A boy brought a white shroud
At five in the afternoon.[11]

Mr. Vivas suggests that Lorca, in this poem, only occasionally speaks directly of his own emotions, but "more often than not, the poem refers to objects and situations directly involved in the death or somehow in the poet's mind connected with it. The expression of the emotion or emotions—for there is, of course, a whole complex of them referred to throughout the poem—is achieved through the presentation of these objects and situations."[12]

In the light of such an analysis, charges like those above against the theory of literature and oral interpretation as emotional expression become unconvincingly simple.

Concerning the oral interpreter's relation to literature, far from striking at his right to interpret emotion, Mr. Vivas' analysis prepares the way for dignifying the interpreter's "expressiveness" into a special obligation. Vivas writes of Lorca's poem that "the man who wrote it is lamenting the death of a bullfighter and that he feels very strongly about that death. One cannot name the emotion he feels by any precise term; and for a good reason, since its full complex specific expression is achieved only through the total poem; but one may loosely refer to it as a desolate sense of loss, a deep and anguishing loss at the death of a great bullfighter whom Garcia Lorca admired greatly."[13] Vivas is surely right: naming the emotional complex in any but the vaguest ways is beyond the powers of criticism. Reproducing that emotional complex is not, however, beyond the scope of an effective oral interpretation. On the contrary, it is perhaps the most important aspect of the interpreter's activity to reproduce this emotional complex in all its specific richness.

Certainly, then, approaching literature by way of its represented objects is not necessarily to deny that emotion

11. From *Creation and Discovery* by Eliseo Vivas (New York: Noonday Press, 1955).
12. Vivas, *Critiques and Essays in Criticism,* p. 395.
13. Ibid.

exists in a piece of literature or that the interpreter has no need to express it. But it does place the matter in a new perspective. If, as Vivas suggests, the emotion which the poem expresses is chiefly dependent on the full assemblage of objects and situations depicted in the poem, we should notice at least three implications of this idea which are of special interest to the oral interpreter.

First, we recognize that the interpreter must closely study the piece in all its relationships. "The full complex specific expression" which it is the interpreter's task to reproduce "is achieved only through the total poem," and the interpreter must regard that total poem — its rhythms, image patterns, connotative elements, etc. — in order to re-embody the complex of emotions.

Second, it is evident that an oral reader who can effectively express the poem's emotions must be a person who is especially sensitive to qualitative aspects of life and literature. He is one who must know the "connections" between objects and emotion, as the connections exist in nature and are represented in new, symbolic forms in literature.

Third, his special function as oral interpreter is to enrich the literary and, we may hope, other life experiences of people who are not so sensitive as himself to qualitative aspects. Of course, people who themselves "understand" literature at the level of its emotional expression can listen to good oral readings with pleasure. Indeed, such persons may well form the interpreter's ideal audience. For such people the interpreter's reading may enrich their own experiences of the piece. But there is another kind of person who can be convinced, one thinks, of the value of literary experience by effective oral reading as apparently he cannot be convinced by the most arduous criticism.

To notice that is not to disparage the excellent service which criticism can, and does, do for literature. As we have seen, effective oral reading and close critical study are intimately related activities. Beyond this, criticism at its best is something more than a mere handmaid to literature. It can be a distinguished "creative" activity in its own right, in that certainly one may point to a number of critical articles which show more intelligence and imagination than a great number of poems which one has read,

To say so much is whole-heartedly to approve the intensively critical approach to literature developed in the classroom, whether in English or oral interpretation, in recent years. But, at the same time, we have some cause to fear that an inordinate stress on critical activity simply produces people who become interested in critical activity rather than in literature.

Reporting on her experience as an editor of *Perspective* magazine, Miss Mona Van Duyn wrote, "To put it . . . concretely, there are at least five times as many people who are interested in reading what someone has to say about certain novels, stories, and poems than there are people who are interested in reading novels, stories, and poems."[14] Accepting Miss Van Duyn's estimate, we need not attribute a deplorable lack of balance in the reading diet simply to the introduction of critical analysis in the classroom. It is sufficient to note that a powerful emphasis on "close" reading has not yet perceptibly increased the affection of the public for serious fiction and poetry.

We should not expect that training in oral interpretation will send future generations rushing to the drug stores for their poetry pocketbooks. If there is a marked deficiency of public interest in serious literature, its cause is very complicated, hardly to be removed by a pedagogical device or two. Still, we should do what we can. The oral interpreter would no more propose "taking literature away" from the critics than good critics would take literature away from the biographers and historians. But the fact remains that oral interpretation has an important part to play in the total attempt to create literary interest and perception. Not wishing to see literature taken from the critics, we should nevertheless like to see it moved on from them, in its neatly catalogued parts, and reassembled in its wholeness in the minds and emotions of readers.

Even while, some years ago, he was calling for a greater critical emphasis in literary study, John Crowe Ransom also

14. Mona Van Duyn, "What's Happening to Prose?" *College English,* XVI (1954), 21.

attested to the value of oral reading: "some of the best work now being done in departments is by the men who do little more than read well aloud, enforcing a private act of appreciation upon the students."[15] Needless to say, whatever one man in one class may do, literary study as a whole is something more inclusive than reading aloud, however well. But we must certainly agree with Mr. Ransom's evaluation of the possibilities for oral reading, though we would extend its practice to students as well as to teachers. Oral interpretation, based on close study of, and sensitive response to, the poetic objects, offers the possibility of conveying with some precision and richness a complex of emotions which can be, as Mr. Vivas suggests, only baldly hinted at by criticism.

We may conclude this chapter by noticing what our analysis does to defend the belief that poetry expresses emotion from charges like those reported above.

First, approaching a poem via its depicted objects does not mean that emotions in poetry are not important. It does mean that they should be understood as intimately related to what the poem "says" or describes, and that they are probably felt fully and precisely only insofar as the whole poem is fully and precisely understood. Furthermore, the emotion that the interpreter projects does not become an unimportant thing in terms of such a theory. On the contrary, when oral interpretation is based on real understanding of the whole piece, and consequently is an accurate re-embodiment of the emotion of the poem, it can perform a unique service in the development of literary experience and perception. And we may well be grateful for the critics of "things" as well as of emotions. It is, at least, the virtue of object-oriented theorists to emphasize the observant regard which poets have for the objects and occasions of our world, as it is the virtue of emotion-oriented critics to emphasize the passion to which his observations have brought the poet and which he can, if *we* are able, communicate to us.

15. Ransom, *The World's Body,* p. 338.

4

THE SOUND, SENSE, AND

PERFORMANCE OF POETRY

We are well aware that the poem comprises not only a semantic structure (on the thematic level, a structure of subjects and meanings; on the expressive or "dramatic" level, a structure of attitudes, actions, and objects) but also a structure of sounds. One of the most evident aspects of sound-structure is poetic meter, the measure of verse by count of syllable or stress. But there are other obviously important aspects of sound-structure — rime, alliteration, assonance, syntactic patterns, juncture (or pause) patterns, and various schemes of phonetic juxtaposition.[1] Professors Wellek and Warren, following certain Russian critics, refer to a number of the sound-effects other than meter as "orchestration,"[2] and for present purposes of analysis we may think of sound-structure as composed of meter and orchestration, including all sound-effects other than meter.

The oral interpreter ordinarily assumes that versification and other aspects of sound-pattern are aspects of, or contribute to, the expressive meanings of the poem. That is, we assume that sound is organically related to sense. But also, as we shall soon note more fully, sound is somehow an independent aspect of poetry, separable from sense. Here, then, I shall try to describe rather fully this seemingly paradoxical condition of

1. For interesting examples of phonetic juxtaposition, see especially Kenneth Burke, *The Philosophy of Literary Form*, rev. ed. (New York: Vintage Books, Inc., 1957), pp. 296-304.
2. René Wellek and Austin Warren, *Theory of Literature* (New York: Harcourt, Brace & Company, 1956), pp. 147-148.

sound in poetry, in order to perceive more fully the relation of oral interpretation to the sound-system of poetry. I will concentrate on the relations of oral reading to the sound-structure of poetry. But the relations discerned should also be roughly those of oral interpretation to prose, in which also sound may be meaningfully patterned, though usually less fully and intricately so than in poetry.

My general conclusion is, from the point of view of the speech man, the entirely orthodox one that the good oral interpretation accurately conveys a poem's sound-structure. The oral interpreter must think of this conclusion as an elementary maxim of his art, or a truism: how could one be a *good* interpreter and *not* communicate so central an aspect of poetry as its sound-structure?

But the oral interpreter emphasizes that a public reading should express a piece's attitudes and actions, that the reader should engage fully with the "dramatic" dimension of the piece. Viewing oral interpretation in that perspective, some sensitive students of literature, including some excellent poets and critics, in effect assert that there is no such thing as *good* oral interpretation.

Or so at least it would appear from Dr. Judith Wray's study of opinions of oral interpretation held by a number of important modern American poets.[3] Several of these excellent writers report simply that they do not want their poems read aloud by trained oral interpreters. Instead, they suggest the value of reading poetry aloud slowly and clearly, and in their own public readings they seem to be careful to maintain a slow tempo and to emphasize metrical stress. To notice their reading in this fashion is to receive a broad hint of the "separable" aspect of sound in poetry. These poets do not merely recommend that poetry be read aloud without particular passion, for "sound alone." Apparently they actually perform in that manner, reading out a separable sound-system.

There are values in such an attitude toward oral reading. The poet who reads aloud dispassionately at least protects

3. Judith Wray, "Theories and Methods of Representative Contemporary Poets as Readers of Their Own Poetry" (Ph.D. abstract), *Speech Monographs*, XXIX, No. 2 (1962), 114-115.

his poem from the "showmanship" of some readings in which the performer's emotional response is only loosely attached to the sense of the poem. Still, this sort of reading is not the most satisfying kind possible. For one thing, a reader cannot read aloud without expressing *some* sort of attitude. He may seem "uninvolved" or "dispassionate" or merely "bored," but whatever he seems, he will seem *something*. Besides, an "attitude-free" reading is one which unnecessarily deprives the poem of its full content and effect: it is pleasant, let us say, to hear the sound of a poem, but one might as well hear its sense too. But, in the context of our present interest, there is a still more severe charge to be brought against the reading that emphasizes only metrical pattern and other sound-effects: we may assert that to read for sound only is to violate the poem's sound!

If we are to understand why this is true, we must analyze both organic and separable aspects of sound and sense, and their bearings on oral interpretation. In order eventually to understand the extent to which an effective oral interpretation conveys the sound-structure of a poem, let us notice first organic relations of sound and sense in poetry. Yvor Winters illustrates this organicity by reference to one of his own verses:

So was the instant blurred;
But as we waited there,
The slow cry of a bird
Built up a scheme of air.[4]

Winters writes as follows of his little quatrain: "The meter is iambic trimeter, and the first, second, and fourth lines are similar in general structure, the first foot of each being reversed, but not heavily, the second and third being normal. The third line departs strongly from this norm, however, and for a purpose. The accented syllables of this line are all heavy and long, the unaccented light and short, so that the feet are clearly marked. The first foot, however, differs

4. From *In Defense of Reason* by Yvor Winters. Copyright 1947, 1960 by Yvor Winters. Reprinted by permission of the publisher, Alan Swallow.

from the first foot of each of the other lines in being iambic, and the second foot differs in being reversed, so that two long and heavy syllables instead of two short and light are brought into juxtaposition. . . . Now the words *slow cry* in this context do not imitate any bird-call known to me, but they suggest the slowness of the cry and the emergence of a definite sound from a surrounding context. The sound apart from the meaning would not have this effect; nor would the sound and meaning of these words alone and apart from the total passage or poem; but I am fairly certain that here they have it."[5]

In Winters' short analysis of his lines we have the case for the organic interdependence of sound and sense put in small compass. However, it would appear that the exact nature of the organic interdependence may vary to some significant extent in different poems. In this poem, for example, we might stress particularly the contribution of metrical variation to the enhancement or vivification of meaning. Of course it is quite true that if the phrase "slow cry" did not actually mean slow cry but something else the sudden stacking up of stressed syllables would not alone remind us of a slow cry. But Winters' example seems not merely to direct our attention in some general way to the organic interdependence of sound and sense, but to the values of variation in meter—in this case, the sudden juxtaposition of strongly stressed syllables, thus dragging and slowing the metrical scheme of the line—to effect or enhance meaning.

In other examples of organicity, our attention may be more fully drawn to the power of meaning to affect or establish the character of sound. Take, for example, the famous lines from Thomas Gray's "Elegy Written in a Country Churchyard":

> The curfew tolls the knell of parting day,
> The lowing herd winds slowly o'er the lea,
> The plowman homeward plods his weary way,
> And leaves the world to darkness and to me.

Professor Gerald Sanders suggests that in the first line

5. Ibid., p. 548.

of this quatrain "long vowels aid in retarding the movement of the lines."[6] If true, it would be one more example of sound's effect in establishing meaning. But the longer we consider the matter, the more likely we are to think that the vowels in the first line are "long" largely because the meaning of the words requires their lengthening. The vowels in the first line are *long* primarily because they happen to be in a context which makes them long: bells, for example, toll *slowly*. Thus, the vowel, like the horse, may be either fast or slow; the kind of spurring given to it by meaning will largely determine the length of the vowel's stride.

On the other hand we could see easily enough in this passage the effect of sound-pattern on meaning. The *tolling,* or slow, aspect of the scene is partly created, or at least emphasized, by the internal alliterative pressure of "tolls . . . knell." Charlton Lewis describes very nicely this power of sound-pattern to emphasize, or corroborate, meaning when he writes, "When you say Titan you mean something big, and when you say tittle you mean something small; but it is not the sound of either word that means bigness or littleness, it is the sense. If you put together a great many similar consonants in one sentence, they will attract special attention to the words in which they occur, and the significance of these words, whatever it may be, is thereby intensified,"[7]

So, in Gray's poem, as in many another, we may think of the effect of sound on meaning as of meaning on sound; but in either case we are giving critical testimony to the organic interdependence of sound and sense.

Rime, too, frequently plays an evident part in establishing a poem's meaning. In his sonnet, "It Is a Beauteous Evening," William Wordsworth begins as follows:

It is a beauteous evening, calm and free,
The holy time is quiet as a Nun
Breathless with adoration; the broad sun
Is sinking down in its tranquility;

6. Gerald Sanders, *A Poetry Primer* (New York: Farrar, Straus and Cudahy, Inc., 1935), p. 21.
7. Quoted by Charles Sears Baldwin, *Ancient Rhetoric and Poetic* (New York: The Macmillan Company, 1924), p. 118.

As many admirers of the poem have noticed, the rimes "nun" and "sun" do some semantic work as well as jingle together.[8] We are forced by the rime to compare the nun with the sun, and so we see the sun itself in a devout and meditative state (and see the nun, perhaps, in a state of "enlightenment"). Of course this sort of rime-embedded metaphor may get out of hand. In this poem, for example, though we are supposed to see the sun in a state of prayerful rapture, doubtless we are not to see the broad sun translated too explicitly into a broad nun! But knowing where to stop relating the terms of a metaphor becomes part of the proper reader's tact. Surely it is because rime can contribute to the full semantic character of a poem that a contemporary poet, Richard Wilbur, says that he likes to use rime because it helps him *think*.[9] That is, hearing an organized noise in his inner ear helps the poet make sense of his poem.

Benjamin Hrushovski puts very well this principle of the organic relations of diverse aspects of poetry when he writes, "A poem cannot be exhaustively decomposed into separate elements, rhythmic, semantic, etc.; to describe the poem we must look at it as a whole from different aspects, the aspect of meaning, the aspect of rhythm, etc. Each of them is but a certain function of the totality of elements of the poem. To use a very simplifying comparison: a poem is like a many-sided crystal; we can observe its inner properties only from one side at a time, but then its whole structure appears through this particular face, showing different emphases in different directions."[10]

In the perspective of Professor Hrushovski's image of the poem as a many-sided crystal, it may be simply argued that the interpreter in expressing accurately the poem's "sense" must also adequately convey its patterns of "sound." The conviction follows hard upon a recognition of the organic relations of the aspects of poetry. If the interpreter is reliably expressing

8. See, for example, Norman F. MacLean, "An Analysis of a Lyric Poem," *The University Review,* VIII (1942), 206-207.
9. Richard Wilbur, "The Genie in the Bottle," *Mid-Century American Poets,* ed. John Ciardi (New York: Twayne Publishers, 1950), pp. 6-7.
10. Benjamin Hrushovski, "On Free Rhythms in Modern Poetry," *Style in Language,* ed. Thomas A. Sebeok (New York: John Wiley & Sons, Inc., 1960), p. 180.

36

attitude and action, it will be because he has grasped them as they have been conditioned or formed by patterns of sound; if he is reliably expressing sound, it will be because he has grasped these effects in their organic relations to sense. Observing in Mr. Winters' quatrain that a "slow cry" must be projected, the interpreter will inevitably convey faithfully the metrical drag at that point in the verse; or, to observe the effect from another facet of the crystal, in expressing the metrical drag, the interpreter will also be suggesting a "slow cry."

I believe that this view of the expert oral interpretation as a communication of organically related sound and sense is, essentially, the true one. But the case for oral interpretation as insightful communication of the sound-structure of poetry is not as self-evident as it might seem from what we have said so far. Hrushovski's statement points to a difficulty. Even while asserting the organic principle, Hrushovski notes a certain independence or separability of the aspects of poetry, as he suggests that we must look at the whole poem from the "different" aspects of meaning and rhythm, etc., or as he suggests that we can observe the "inner properties" of a poem "only from one side at a time." Here Hrushovski is referring to the critic's need to perceive the whole poem one aspect at a time. But the separability of sound from sense, in some fashion and to some extent, may be seen as an intrinsic characteristic of the poem itself. Professors Wimsatt and Beardsley, for example, suggest that one of the central "propositions" of a classic or traditionalist account of English meter is this: "The meter of a line is verifiable in the same sense as the pronunciation of its words is discovered in a dictionary, or by the lexicographer himself. Indeed, there may be meter in nonsense lines, if most of the syllables in these lines are recognized as combinations of English phonemes and are approximate morphemes, subject to acknowledged rules of stressing or leaving unstressed (everyone knows how to pronounce 'sporkling warkle')."[11] Presumably then we could identify the meter of a line, and in some measure recite it

11. W. K. Wimsatt, Jr., and M. C. Beardsley, "The Concept of Meter: an Exercise in Abstraction" (abstract), *Style in Language,* pp. 193-194.

faithfully, even though we did not know the meanings of all or even many of the words in the line.

Surely it is true that in some fashion sound *is* separable from sense in poetry. Taught to pronounce a foreign language which otherwise we do not understand, we may at once identify, and quite easily read aloud, various aspects of sound-structure. Imagine, for example, a person who can pronounce German but does not know the meaning of many, or any, German words. Such a reader may nevertheless quite confidently grasp the metrical pattern of a German poem and easily identify rimes and many other effects of "orchestration."

One of the most interesting "proofs" of the independent status, or separability, of sound-structure is offered by Wimsatt and Beardsley. Their argument is especially convincing because it derives from analysis of a critic who himself shows the significant extent to which sound and meaning are organically related.

In his *Practical Criticism,* I. A. Richards wishes to show, as Wimsatt and Beardsley put it, that "the movement or rhythm of poetry is closely interdependent with its other kinds of meaning." To do so, Richards sets up a metrical "double or dummy," a "purified dummy" as Richards calls it, replete with "nonsense syllables." Richards' dummy verse goes like this:

> J. Drootan-Sussting Benn
> Mill-down Leduren N.
> Telama-taras oderwainto weiring
> Awersey zet bidreen
> Ownd intellester sween.[12]

"If any reader," says Richards, "has any difficulty in scanning these verses, reference to Milton, *On the Morning of Christ's Nativity, XV,* will prove of assistance."[13] Richards makes his point clearly enough. Even if we are not fond of Milton's *Nativity,* we are likely to think it substantially supe-

12. From *Practical Criticism* (1950) by I. A. Richards. Reprinted by permission of Harcourt, Brace & World, Inc., New York.
13. I. A. Richards, *Practical Criticism* (New York: Harcourt, Brace & Company, 1950), p. 232.

rior to J. Drootan-Sussting Benn, poor fellow, all Mill-down Leduren N.

Or Richards would *seem* to make his point clearly enough. Eager to distinguish seeming from being, Wimsatt and Beardsley argue convincingly that Richards' dummy illustrates beautifully a point he had no wish to make: that at least one aspect of the sound-system, to wit meter, actually exists as a separable aspect of the poem. Wimsatt and Beardsley argue cogently that, whatever Richards intended, his is certainly not a *pure* dummy. They question, "How could it be? It was a linguistic dummy. And so this dummy did have meter — perhaps even a kind of rhythm. If it did not have a meter, how could it be adduced as showing that quality? And if you can do that, you prove that the quality can be isolated — at least from *certain* other qualities. In this case, from the *main lines* of the linguistic meaning. In order to get even this dummy of a meter, Richards had to leave in a good many linguistic features." Then Wimsatt and Beardsley enumerate some of the plainly identifiable features of sound which Richards has separated from meaning. "Let us list some of the things we know about this dummy. The 'nonsense' syllables are divided into groups (i.e., words). As English readers we find little difficulty pronouncing them. Some of the groups are English words (*mill, down*); others are English syllables, even morphemes (*ing, ey, een, er*). The rhymes give us very strong indications, absolutely sure indications, where some of the stresses must fall. And there are some syllables, notably some final syllables, which are surely unstressed."[14] Wimsatt and Beardsley list still other identifiable elements of sound, but we have cited enough such features to show that they ground a solid case for the separability of meter from meaning. It would seem to follow by reasonable extension of the argument of these writers that those parts of the sound-system which we have called effects of orchestration are also separable. Certainly it is easy enough to identify separately, without considerations of meaning or semantic reference, patterns of recurrence in letters, syllables, phrase-lengths, etc.

14. W. K. Wimsatt, Jr., and M. C. Beardsley, "The Concept of Meter: an Exercise in Abstraction," *PMLA*, LXXIV (1959), 590-591.

In showing the separability of sound from sense, Wimsatt and Beardsley in no way suggest that sound is not more effective when organically related to sense. Like us, surely, these critics prefer Milton's verse to Richards' dummy. But the question is not merely one of greater or lesser effect, but the relation of the separable sound-structure to the actual sound of the poem; are these one and the same thing?

I believe that they are not. We may indeed separate sound from sense in that we may identify properties of sound-structure apart from consideration of semantic reference, or meaning. But in withdrawing sound from sense we also withdraw it from sound. That is, the sound-structure which we can identify as a separable system is not *all* of the poem's sound-structure, but a part of it — and a portion which is in qualitative terms, as Richards' dummy shows, singularly uninteresting.

Such a view of separable sound as but a part of the total sound-structure of the poem derives inevitably from recognition of the principle of organic form in poetry. In the case of the semantics of a poem, its "meaning" or "sense," the critics of our time are in widespread agreement. Of course we can in some measure separate, or withdraw or abstract, sense from the whole poem. For one purpose or another we frequently paraphrase a poem — we try to boil away from the poem all but its semantic system or sense. In making the paraphrase we testify to our belief that sense is in some degree a separable element. But we are fully warned that the meanings of our paraphrases are a pale reflection of the total meaning actually embodied in the poem. That is, the separable sense — the sense which we can identify in our paraphrases — is a sickly residue of the total poem, not only because the sense which we identify in our paraphrases is a withdrawal of sense from sound but because it is also a withdrawal of sense from sense. The sense of our paraphrases, we are well agreed, is but a portion of the sense of the whole poem, only an aspect of the full meaning.

Cleanth Brooks, for example, points out that we cannot state in abstract language — in that "other" language of paraphrase — even the full thematic content or symbolic sig-

40

nificance of the poem.[15] Doubtless that is, precisely, true. We understand the poem to be a representation of a complex of actions, attitudes, and objects in which, frequently, thematic meanings are but implicitly embedded. Or if themes are explicitly stated within the poem, they "grow out of" or derive from the represented actions and attitudes within the poem. Since it is the words of the poem that give us the actions and attitudes and objects in their exactitude, the changed words of our paraphrases inevitably change the character of the dramatic complex and so, inevitably, of its thematic implications. But perhaps we can at least come *close* to rendering fully, in the other language of paraphrase, thematic meanings and symbolic extensions of reference. Literary critics at least must believe so. On such a faith depends the value of exegesis and criticism. But poetic "meaning," in the broadest sense, includes not only themes and ideas but the whole expressive dimension of the poem, of attitude, actions, and properties of objects. As we have seen, these expressive and expressible qualities are in part semantic evocations and are in part built up through the play of the sound-system on meaning as in, for example, the slow cry of Mr. Winters' bird. Obviously only the poem, in its total configuration of sound and word, can give us the expressive or "dramatic" meaning of the poem.

If then one observes the relationship of separable sound to the whole poem, one sees readily enough that the same relationship prevails as in the case of separable or paraphrasable sense. In the case of sense, paraphrase communicates a *part* of the semantic system, or sense, of the whole of a poem. In the case of sound, whether we identify a separable sound-system visually, by markings and counting, or by reading the lines, aloud or *sotto voce*, without *particular* attitude or passion, we are identifying only a portion of the sound-system as it exists in the whole poem in its relation to the semantic system. We may put it this way: whatever Mr. Richards thought he was doing, Professors Wimsatt and Beardsley discovered in his poetic dummy isolable sound-values of a poem. But in the view taken here, whatever else Wimsatt

15. Cleanth Brooks, *The Well Wrought Urn* (New York: Harcourt, Brace & Company, 1947); see especially pp. 67, 180.

and Beardsley may be doing, in pointing to isolable sound-values they are but making a "paraphrase," or contributing to some possible paraphrase, of the actual sound-values of the poem.

We may summarize relations between the separable and organically whole sound-system as follows. The sound of a poem consists of a separable or an *abstract* sound-structure and an *actual* sound-structure. The abstract sound-structure consists of those metrical and orchestrational effects which, generally speaking, may be identified irrespective of considerations of meaning. We do not need to know the meaning of "sporkling warkle" to know that the phrase consists of two trochaic feet; neither would we need to know the meanings of "glom" and "bom" to know that, in a certain relation to one another within lines of verse, they would rime.

But we should also notice that the abstract sound-system is but a part of the actual sound-system. That is not the same thing as to say that the actual sound-system "fulfills" the abstract sound-system. To talk in such a fashion would seem to imply that the abstract sound-system resides in the poem as a separable Platonic model which the reader can only approximate in some more-or-less shadowy way. But the shadows lie in quite the opposite direction. It is the separable sound-system which, until it is transfused with sense, lies bodiless in the shadows. Of course we may if we wish speak of the actual sound of the poem "fulfilling" the abstract sound-system, but we should know that we mean by such a statement only what we would mean were we to say that the meaning of the poem-as-a-whole "fulfills" a paraphrase of content. It would appear to be more precise to say that the abstract sound-system "contributes" to, or is a portion of, the actual sound-system.

Consider, for example, one line of a poem written in a metrical pattern of iambic pentameters (from Alexander Pope's "An Essay on Criticism"):

And ten low words oft creep in one dull line.

As Seymour Chatman remarks, one determinant of the

42

full sound of this line is the stress-level of these words in "normal non-verse speech." But the metrical pattern, as pattern, also exerts a pressure on the sound-structure, so that the stresses of the words "low" and "dull" are "suppressed" by the abstract meter because of their position between "theoretical metrical stress points." Professor Chatman refers to the overlapping, or even contradictory, pressures of the sound of a word in non-verse speech and metrical pattern as a "metrical tension," and he would seem entirely accurate in his perception. But also we may note still another pressure on the poem's sound-system, deriving from the expressive or "attitudinal" system of the poem. Both "low" and "dull," though they may be "suppressed" by metrical pattern, are surely "heightened" (or in Chatman's word "promoted"[16]) by their dramatic significances, their meanings, in the context of line and poem.

There is something amusing in my example, for surely it would be easier to approximate the "actual" sound of this line, in some reading or another, than to account fully for the factors of its structure, so tremblingly full of "tension." Still, though we have cited but one line of a poem, and with respect to that line have spoken only of its metrical aspects, it is an evident example of the view that the actual sound-system of a poem is the "larger," "fuller" system in the sense that the abstract sound-system is but one of its aspects. The actual sound-system will include also the dramatic or expressive and even thematic effects of the poem, and possibly be conditioned still further by the memory of the usual stress of words as they occur in non-verse "conversational" speech. The actual sound-system will be the sound of the poem as it is organically determined by the play on one another of abstract sound-system and dramatic, or semantic, system.

Now the abstract sound-system of a poem is readily identifiable. We say, for example, of such-and-such a poem that it is written in iambic pentameter, that it has a rime scheme of abab, cdcd, etc., and that it is chock-full of liquid l's. But how do we identify the actual sound-system? Where do we find it?

16. Seymour Chatman, "Robert Frost's 'Mowing': An Inquiry into Poetic Structure," *Discussions of Poetry: Rhythm and Sound,* ed. George Hemphill (Boston: D. C. Heath & Company, 1961), pp. 84-85.

The *perfectly* correct answer to this question would appear to be that the *actual* sound-system of a poem is an ideal structure. Isn't that an interestingly queer way of putting it? But to put it so does not mean that the actual sound-system exists nowhere.

At one level of understanding we may say that the actual sound-system exists, as rhythm exists for Professor Hrushovski, "as an 'auditory imagination.'"[17] It is an *ideal* structure in the sense that such a structure would be the system or rhythm which caught perfectly and fully expressed all possible relations between dramatic meaning and abstract sound-structure.

Well, man is a stubborn creature who would make his ideals come true. Thus we find approximate realizations of the actual, or ideal, sound-structure. I imagine the perfecting reader of poetry, reading a poem, *sotto voce* or to the "inner ear," dread chasm, many times to himself. My imagination carries me only so far: most of his readings, as I must think of them, are disasters, happily for his good name kept at home. But I am able to imagine some good readings amid the bilge he pumps into his inner ear and to imagine further that these readings help correct one another until my perfecting reader's awareness of the actual sound-system is a complex "auditory imagination" of his best readings put somehow almost together.

I imagine too another kind of listener to the sound of poetry. He is the expertly attentive listener to oral readings, and so (let us say) he attends several performances of the same poem by different public readers. And he too puts some good performances — though these are the performances of persons other than himself — together in his auditory imagination to grasp, almost, the actual sound of the poem.

Such a view of the matter should do much to comfort persons like Professor Hrushovski who regretfully notes that "a full realization of the rhythm by voice reading is often impossible."[18] Indeed, that is so, and it is also true that a full realization of the rhythm by silent reading is often impossible.

17. Hrushovski, p. 181.
18. Ibid.

Meantime, readers of poetry must manfully do what they can. Thus we need not insist on too much perfection but only on its mystery. Our interest here is in the oral interpreter, and the relation of his interpretation to the actual sound-system of the poem. From what we have said I think it is clear that we may think of an oral interpretation as that which approximates the actual sound of the poem.

Recall, for example, Robert Burns's rose. In reading "My love is like a red red rose," doubtless the interpreter will seek to suggest the special vividness of object and feeling implicit in the repetition of "red." Such matters comprise the expressive meaning of the line, and in reading it we will wish to communicate that meaning if possible. Later I shall suggest at least one way in which the interpreter might "voice" the line to express its attitude or meaning. But were we to change the focus of our attention only a little, we would see that in attempting to communicate the precise attitude of the line we are greatly affecting the sound-pattern of the poem. The sounding of the vowel, the pause, and of course the whole speed and tempo of the line are geared to the attitude or meaning which we would express.

This is to say that, in reading so, the oral interpreter is communicating the sound-structure *of* or *in* the line. The exact expressive weight of the syllables and pausing are required because the *meaning* of the line requires just such a weighting. We only know accurately the sound-system of a poem when it is charged with attitude and meaning, just as we only know fully the semantic system when it is charged with sound.

It is well enough to say, then, that oral interpretation approximates the actual sound of the poem. But oral interpretation must be produced, alas, by oral interpreters, and various interpreters read the same poem aloud in various ways. Indeed, the same interpreter may seldom (let us say, considering his various readings or performances precisely, that he will never) read the same poem twice in the same way. What are we to make of these differences? Have we reached some irreducible paradox—that oral interpretation approximates the actual sound of the poem but that oral interpreters treat the actual sound as if it were an infinitely variable thing?

It is of course some such fear which motivates the poet who guards the expressive freight of meaning in his poem by reading it monotonously. (I am speaking of the poet who reads with a monotonous chant on principle and not merely because he is unskillful.) It is this concern which causes Professor Hrushovski to say that voice reading cannot convey the full realization of a poem's rhythm because "there are in reading subjective elements."[19] Such poets and critics, detecting differences among oral interpretations, do not wish to encourage the view that a poem is anything its reader wishes.

Professors Wimsatt and Beardsley put very well what seems to them the risk run by a poem in its oral interpretation: "A poem, as verbal artifact or complex linguistic entity, is, to be sure, actualized or realized in particular performances of it—in being read silently or aloud. But the poem itself is not to be identified with any performance of it or with any subclass of performances; that is to say, not everything that a reader does to the poem in speaking it is a property of the poem itself: a speaker with a Southern accent and a speaker with a Western accent give different readings but are reading the same poem."[20] Doubtless, in a comic mood, one may discover in this way of putting things some unconscious humor. Wimsatt and Beardsley may seem to be saying, at bottom, that if we are to understand or "realize" a poem, that "complex entity," we must read it or hear it read. Surely that is so, but must we really regret the fact since readers are bound to be Southerners or Westerners or even something less universal in scope? We may be led even to ponder the wonderful, profitless question whether a Southerner, for example, must read a poem even silently with a Southern accent. Still, it is doubtless best for us to take this passage with full seriousness and sympathy. Obviously, whatever else they may intend, these critics do not mean to stress reading performance as that which conveys something *in* the poem but as that which does something *to* it. And we may think that they do so because they wish to make certain that we will not confuse the nature of a poem with the personal responses of its readers.

19. Ibid.
20. Wimsatt and Beardsley, *Style in Language*, p. 193.

46

Anxieties of this sort are produced in behalf of a good cause, for a poem has an intrinsic being. Though his passions may have been aroused as deeply as a lover's by a poem, its proper reader embraces the poem, not himself, and he embraces it not to improve it but to know it. But the fact of differences among oral interpretations, properly understood, does not challenge but deeply supports such a view of the poem as an object in itself and of its proper reader as an honest lover.

What I mean is this. Differences exist among oral interpretations of the same piece. That is a fact. But we should not see these differences as all of the same sort to be attributed to a single cause — the unreigned subjectivity of responses on the part of neighing readers. Some differences do indeed derive from qualities of the person: as Wimsatt and Beardsley suggest, if an interpreter speaks with a regional accent, it will surely affect the "sound" he produces in reading a poem. So too it will affect the sound if he has a "high" voice or a "low" one, a generally relaxed intonational pattern or a generally tense one. And so forth. Shortly I shall suggest that even these differences in interpretations deriving from differences among persons may be of different sorts, and few of them, so long as they are understood for what they are, really harmful violations of the poem. Now I mean merely to remark that for the critic to concentrate on differences deriving from personal qualities of the interpreter is to miss the most significant sort of differences among oral interpretations.

The most significant difference is a qualitative one. Simply, some readings are better than others. We have seen that an oral interpretation approximates the actual sound of the poem. It remains to be said explicitly that the more skillful in performance is the interpreter, the more fully he knows his poem, the more closely will his reading approximate the actual sound of the poem. Or, to put the matter without qualification, among different readings of the same poem some are better, or closer approximations, than others. That will be true whether one is speaking of different readings of a poem considered as a whole, or of readings considered in relation to the poem's actual sound-system, including abstract metrical and orchestrational elements, organically related to sense.

47

The fundamental ground for such a view of qualitative differences must be experience rather than theory. One has either had the experience of hearing a poem more fully "sounded" by one interpreter than another or one has not. Or to put it in terms of the performer's perspective, one either does or does not have the experience of thinking one of his readings or "performances" of a poem, whether to others or himself, superior to some other of his readings in reflecting the whole poem, the full sound-system. Or he may have had the experience of thinking his reading of some part of the poem superior to some other of his readings of that part, be it word, line, or stanza.

We may find in that brilliant amateur, Thomas Jefferson (a political man accustomed to handling matters of endless dispute diplomatically), a remarkably suggestive statement of the experience of excellence. Discussing English poetry, Jefferson in a short passage vividly illuminates the central matters we have been discussing — the distinction between abstract and actual sound-systems and oral interpretation as proximate performance of the actual sound of the poem. Jefferson writes, "Though there be accents on the first, the second, or the third syllables of the foot, as has been before explained, yet is there a subordination among these accents, a modulation in their tone of which it is impossible to give a precise idea in writing. This is intimately connected with the sense; and though a foreigner will readily find to what words that would give distinguished emphasis, yet nothing but habit can enable him to give actually the different shades of emphasis which his judgment would dictate to him. Even natives have very different powers as to this article. This difference exists both in the organ and the judgment. Foote is known to have read Milton so exquisitely that he received great sums of money for reading him to audiences who attended him regularly for that purpose."[21] The image of a man reading aloud for great sums of money is bound to enrapture the oral interpreter. But how definitely it is Mr. Foote of whom Jefferson is speaking. It is not just *any* interpreter but Mr.

21. Thomas Jefferson, from "Thoughts on English Prosody," *Discussions of Poetry: Rhythm and Sound*, p. 23.

48

Foote who knew not only what syllables to tap, but just how hard to tap them in order to turn them from sleeping to waking beauties.

Once one has heard an excellent reader, or has almost been, if only during the utterance of a line or two, an excellent reader, theoretical considerations will seem perhaps self-evident. The chief theoretical ground for identifying Mr. Foote's performance as qualitatively superior to others is the theory of the poem as a complex entity of intrinsic properties. That is most interesting. Critics like Hrushovski, Wimsatt, and Beardsley, noticing differences among performances, fear oral interpretation as subjective expression. Now, as we have seen, differences do exist. But only a view of the poem like that held by the aforementioned critics permits us to evaluate the differences in relation to the poem so that, like Jefferson, we may say that Mr. Foote better than anyone else produces the actual sound of Milton's poem. If the poem is but some sort of linguistic stimulus to emotion, we may talk about Foote's performance as performance but not of his performance of Milton. Without this theory of the poem we could have no standards — beyond a few gross measures such as "more" or "less" emotional response — for evaluating performance of a poem or parts of a poem (two readers may read various parts with various excellence). But if a poem is an entity, an organic being having its own "life" or being its own "world," then the poem itself becomes the measure of value in performance. A performance is "good" or "bad" in the measure to which it does or does not illumine the poem. Let us put the matter contrastively: Wimsatt and Beardsley suggest (quite accurately) that "not everything that a reader does to the poem in speaking it is a property of the poem itself." Here, we are simply emphasizing that many a thing a reader "does" to the poem in speaking it *may* be a property of the poem itself. Put more precisely, what the performer *does* may well illumine, make clear, properties of the poem itself. If the oral interpreter does illumine properties of the poem itself, he has performed more effectively, he has given a "better" reading, than the interpreter who does not illumine the poem or does so but murkily. I am speaking of the relation of oral inter-

49

pretation to the whole poem. But also, obviously, I am speaking simultaneously of the relation of oral interpretation to the actual sound, organic tissue of abstract sound-system and semantic system, of the poem.

Let me now imagine a generous reader of these pages, prepared to believe that an oral interpreter is one who tries to read poems well and not merely express himself. Still, such a generous reader might well think that we have offered small proof indeed of qualitative differences among readings in saying that the poem itself is the measure or standard of evaluation of various performances. For who knows the poem itself? How can we measure a thing if we can't find the yardstick?

The absolute answer to a question of this sort is that nobody, not even its author, knows the poem itself. Or let us put it, like a German philosopher, that only the poem knows the poem itself—and then add to that, like a British empiricist, that the poem couldn't care less.

But this does not mean that the poem cannot be known. The poem can be known approximately and provisionally, which is to say that the answer to what the poem is cannot be discovered in a computing machine. Some elements of a faith in the computer would seem to motivate much contemporary linguistic analysis of poetry and the relations to it of oral reading. Professor Chatman, for example, inquiring into the prosodic structure of Robert Frost's poem, "Mowing," studied eight different tape-recorded oral performances of it by eight readers. None of these readers claimed "any special elocutionary talent," according to Chatman, "and no great search for talented readers was made, since the very purpose of the analysis was to describe the room for variation in performance that any poem presumably allows, even in a random selection of readers."[22] Now, we should wish to praise attempts like Mr. Chatman's to discover what insight into prosodic structure may be afforded by oral performance. The interest of the linguistic analyst of poetry in the many small differences in pausing, phrasing, and stressing on the part of various readers must seem to the oral interpreter an altogether praiseworthy thing. But praising a critical interest in even minute individ-

22. Chatman, p. 85

50

ual differences in performance is a very different thing from thinking that we shall learn much about a poem simply by listening to the reading of a poem by a "random selection of readers." Mr. Chatman wants to make room for variation in performance that any poem allows. Good enough; but to do so he must find *good* readers who will know what the poem allows. Bad readers make their own allowances. If they are bad enough they may even read the poem backwards, if they choose, and listening to them we have often wished that they had done so. Thus, if the poem is an entity of intrinsic properties, it does *not* provide for the variations expressed by a random selection of readers; whatever randomly selected readers may "do" with it, the poem itself provides only for those variations which reflect various of its intrinsic properties. The most probable consequence of studying eight random oral readers is that one will be attending eight rancid performances.

But Professor Chatman is a keen student of poetry whose respect for the art happily undoes his theory of random selection of readers. One of the eight readers whom he studied was the author of the poem, and Chatman reports, "I must confess that one or two passages were clarified for me when I analyzed the junctural features of Frost's performance."[23] Doubtless there is no need to confess to having received the gift of fresh insight, but surely Chatman is right to remark the reader's "sounding" that provides it. Since not all of the noises made by his eight readers are equally worth noting, Chatman does well to comment on those which return him to knowledge of the poem itself. And of course Professor Chatman did not *really* make a random selection of readers, for all of them were "professional teachers of literature."[24] Presumably, then, whether or not they were capable of expressing it orally, and thus making it available to others, these readers had some special insight into the actual sound of the poem. Perhaps the full value of a theory of learning something about the nature of poetry by listening to random performances of it can only be envisioned when we have entrusted a text for reading to eight fully committed logical positivists.

23. Ibid., p. 88.
24. Ibid., p. 85.

You will understand that I am not suggesting that a "bad" reading may not nevertheless reveal properties of the poem itself. But a *perfectly* bad reading would not reveal anything of the poem, and where a reading does reveal properties of the poem itself it will not be so bad. My point is not that bad reading may not teach us something about the poem, but that the poem must teach us something about bad reading. We cannot come to know the poem by simply totaling up what a lot of performances "do" to it, but we can evaluate the lot of performances as we come to know the poem — and it is no paradox to be told that listening to good performance, or working ourselves toward good performance, is among the ways by which we come to know the poem.

I am but saying once more that which has been said, or assumed, many times before by critics, that the poem is a world to be discovered, and that we discover it as fully as we can by sharing our insights into it. The person who asks how we may know a poem asks a proper question, but he must be content that the oral interpreter can answer it only like any other student of literature. We learn what we can and we help one another learn.

In the case of literary criticism we are reasonably well agreed on what we can and cannot expect from it. Many things are said by various persons about the poem, and it is a mystery indeed why some of these things seem to us meaningful about the poem and other things said to not seem meaningful about the poem. And there is no one in the vicinity to tell us with absolute surety whether we are right or wrong to think meaningful the critical comment of which we approve as yielding fresh insight into the poem. But this is a mystery we live with fairly happily, unless we are philosophers, and it in no way disturbs our faith that the poem really *is,* and that some critical comment, or some of our own impressions, may reveal more of what the poem really is than still other comment or other impressions.

The same situation prevails in oral interpretation. One good reading does not preclude another, even a strikingly different one, of the same poem. But each of these readings will be "good" insofar as it reveals aspects of the poem.

52

Parallels in the relations to the poem of oral interpretation and literary criticism — or in any event literary exegesis — are many, and fairly exact. Some differences, whether in oral or written interpretation, may more nearly reflect qualities of the interpreter than of the poem. In the case of the oral interpreter, for example, we have seen that his expression of sound may well reflect qualities of his person — his regional accent, if he has one, the timbre of his voice, even his usual emotional state, etc. But the critical writer, too, very likely expresses an individualistic critical "manner." We are unlikely to mistake an essay by Edmund Wilson for one by Ezra Pound. In the case of written comment, we may well enjoy, or dislike, a critical manner, thought of as a thing-in-itself. But we have no difficulty distinguishing between, say, Eliot's expression of himself and those aspects of his essay which are insights into the work he is investigating.

Ordinarily we assume that the critical manner is an expression of the personal perspective within which the critic can see the work. It is a "frame" for his criticism or elucidation in that it defines the limits within which his perceptions can occur, be valid. That, too, is how we should understand the personal signature of the oral interpreter's performance. Given such a view, it is hard even to admit the possibility that some given poem should not be read by some given oral interpreter on the grounds that his vocal apparatus simply cannot accommodate its meanings but only torment it with an alien personality. Rather, we would understand the particular personality, the particular voice, as the frame, aesthetically more-or-less neutral, within which the interpreter's intelligent variations express the meanings, the actual sound of the poem. Indeed, a woman can splendidly act the role of Hamlet: the unmistakable feminine timbre of her voice rapidly becomes a thing of aesthetic indifference to the audience; it is the frame within which she delivers the expressive, authentic voice of Hamlet. Still, the timbre of her voice *is* a frame, and she can deliver only those possibilities of Hamlet's character which can be revealed within such a frame.

So we may say, then, that some differences in either written or oral interpretation, though more-or-less interesting in themselves, are not to be thought of as critically meaningful but as personal signatures. Granted, in oral interpretation the personal signature, the things a reader does to the poem as an act of personality merely, may be so compelling that we hardly care (for a time) whether the interpretation reveals the poem, so fascinatingly does it reveal the interpreter. But the critical writer's personality, too, may overwhelm and be the most interesting revelation of his "analysis": who, for example, would really read H. L. Mencken for his insight into literature?

And there are other parallels to report. There can be, indeed, more than one good oral interpretation of the same poem. But in the case of criticism, because we have had one good critical paper on *Hamlet* does not mean that another cannot be written. The same oral interpreter may read the same poem in rather strikingly different ways. But the literary critic, too, may well change his stride significantly in his second essay on a given poet, and still have made sense in both essays. Some mediocre oral interpretations may nevertheless reveal *something* of a poem, its metrical scheme, for example; but, in literary criticism, not even student papers may be safely ignored, even by professors. And so forth.

Surely we must, out of hope rather than despair, accept differences, whether in oral or written interpretation, as profitable mysteries. The poem, full of secret panels and queerly reflecting mirrors, is an enchanted as well as an enchanting country. We identify the expert oral interpreter and the expert literary critic only as we do Kilroy — something in our own experience, however fragile and incomplete, of the queer country tells us that they were really there. If they offer to guide us through the poem on one more tour, we are lucky indeed if we have reason to think the trip worth making.

5

NOTE ON POETS' RECORDED
READINGS OF THEIR OWN WORKS

The poet, we have said, despite his creative talent, may have a poor understanding of what it means to read a poem well aloud. But that does not mean that we should ignore the oral readings of poets on principle, even when they are poor readers. Instead, we may think, there are particular values in the readings by poets of, at least, their own works.

Notice, for example, the conclusion of Lee Anderson. Mr. Anderson has performed one of the most interesting, and valuable, services in behalf of poetry of any contemporary man of letters. For many years Anderson moved back and forth across the United States, recording poets of known or possible significance, and the recordings he made are now housed at Yale University, which is slowly producing a series of records of these poets' readings. Anderson says of poetry readings, "In the teaching of poetry the most useful function of oral interpretation of poems is in determination of *tone*. Tone is a key word in criticism and instruction. . . . A poem read aloud, or heard on a record, will tell us more about attitude and tone than any number of readings by eye. I use the device of listening in my recording-of-poets at work. It enables me to distinguish the real from the pseudo more quickly and easily. Before an invitation is given to a poet to record for Yale I read some of the poet's work to tape. The tape playback is my touchstone for judgment."[1]

1. Lee Anderson, "How Not to Read Poems—A Dissenting View," *Art and the Craftsman,* ed. Joseph Harned and Neil Goodwin (Carbondale, Ill.: Southern Illinois University Press, 1962) p. 211.

According to Anderson, then, it would seem that the poet's reading of his own work is in some measure a touchstone of its quality. Today there are available many recordings of literature, of poetry and fiction, by professional interpreters and actors as well as by poets. Listening alertly and critically to these recordings can be highly rewarding to the student of oral interpretation. But there are some special pleasures in listening to poets reading their own works. Yale University and the Library of Congress in particular have made the poets' readings available to the public, and in doing so they have assured for modern poetry a spoken anthology of unique values. Let us, as a suggestion of some of the things which make these records matters of interest to the student of oral interpretation, note some of these values.

One of them will embarrass most of our poets, as their voices sow rumors of their personalities and characters. But how, unless we hear him dressed in his own personal voice, will we guess that Mr. Wheelock (Library of Congress recording) really does sound like Orson Welles? Or guess that Stephen Vincent Benét (Library of Congress) may well have been a tough, taut man? Or how, otherwise, shall we take a certain small pleasure in hearing John Hollander's (Yale recordings) cool round tones break suddenly with a disarmingly anxious youthful inflection? The "pure" reader will acknowledge to his pure poet that these are extraneous pleasures—and insist on enjoying them nevertheless. Healthily coarse, we are interested in the poet, and there are times when we do not wish to take our minds off him. *Ethos,* that queerly permanent word out of the old Greek rhetorics, is a quality of person rather than of composition. And as we hear the voice, whirling off the grooves of its permanent record, we weigh (whether we will or not) the man behind the poem.

But of course what the poet wishes us to hear, and what we in our critical integrity strive to hear, is the *authentic* voice of the poem. The authentic voice will give us fresh insight into the poem, or reinforce such insight as we already may have had. And the poet, reading his own poem, cannot fail in authenticity—even though his triumph be nature's gift rather than an art of speech.

I touch on a simple mystery. I mean that even if the poet is not a professionally expert oral interpreter, his voice may nevertheless awaken, or reawaken, our sense of important qualities in his poetry. Take the Edwin Muir-Stephen Vincent Benét record (Library of Congress) as a revealing example. Neither poet reads badly. On the other hand, it is hard to imagine either of them being hounded to read anybody *else's* poetry. Yet neither man can help knowing, in important measure, how to read his own verses.

With Muir, we enjoy at once the personal voice, burry and Scotch, the rich country accents of Orkney. We would enjoy hearing *that* voice, or another generally like it, reading from the telephone book. But soon enough we hear the essential voice that directs us to qualities of the poetry. In Muir this is a quiet, enduring voice, gentle though not cheerful, fearing nothing but exaggerated emphasis. And as we listen to Muir, and read his poetry, and listen and read yet again, I think we come to feel that none other could capture quite so well the central tonal achievement—and even constructive principle—of his poetry.

Muir's reading emphasizes something that perhaps we should know already about the tone and structure of his poetry. Benét thrusts on our attention qualities we did not know, or had almost forgotten, he possesses. Of course his readings are vibrant and dramatic, full of the ballader's stomp and hoy, as we would have expected from the man said to have put *Gone with the Wind* into verse. But there is another tone we might not have expected—something tense, grinding, and tough. It is almost *too* much; at time Benét's are the hard, bitter tones of honest Sam Spade saying no to the Dark Lady. Still, those tones re-create for us what is truly *in* the poetry— the poet's full sense, beneath all the dramatic pyrotechnics and even sentimentalities, of just how hard and unyielding life is and must be, and of the hard realism required to confront and, in a measure, to triumph over it. His reading led me, at least, to a rediscovery of significant aspects of Benét's poetry.

And so we may receive revealing clues from other poets. For example, W. D. Snodgrass may well be the poetic model *par excellence* of the man to whom things happen—and the voice of the poet (Library of Congress) appropriately embodies the special nervous bewilderment of the modern pawn of populations and of states. There is too John Ciardi's dirge-like tone of muffled anger (Library of Congress) or Robert Hillyer's voice (Library of Congress), remote and nostalgic, to enhance our realizations of important thematic dimensions of their poetry, and so on through the list of these appropriately, and somewhat surprisingly, singular voices.

But as our attention slowly shifts from the voice of the speaker *of* the poem to that of the speaker, or speakers, *in* the poem, our demands for authenticity become more strict. We want to hear not only clues and hints, however rich, but the full artistic life of the poem. Few poets, to put the matter plainly, can thus fully perform their own poems. The situation should surprise us no more than in the case of the playwright acting in his own plays. He may be Noel Coward but he is still more likely to be silent Cal, or even Charles, the wrestler.

Let me illustrate by reference to Muir, whom I have already justly commended. Take the first poem he reads on his Library of Congress record, "The Animals." As a poem it is a splendid evocation of imaginative participation in timeless innocence, whose emblem is the "animals," counterpointed against a sharp, decisive sense of careworn human history. But Muir does not make this experience real for us in his recorded reading. But we may suppose that an oral reading performed with fullest art and effectiveness *could* re-create the little miracle of parallel experiences enacted within the poem itself.

I have said that the speech artist will give us the whole poem. In the perspective of its oral performance, the whole poem is, as we have seen, easily described. It consists of an abstract sound-complex and a semantic-complex, organically related. For "sound" we may substitute as rough equivalents "rhythmic" or "metric"; for "semantic" we may read "attitude" or "dramatic" or even "emotion." The oral interpreter's task is, while rendering each fully, to project these two systems, of sounds and "meanings," in harmonious relation with one another and with the artistic purpose or purposes of the poem.

We may generalize that poets reading their own works are best at preserving the abstract sound-complex. Maxwell Bodenheim (Library of Congress) is one charming exception to this rule: reading aloud with obvious delight and dramatic energy, he nevertheless phrases and emphasizes words most oddly, like a reader who keeps losing his place in the text. It may well be that, during his recording, that is exactly what happened to him.

Let Vernon Watkins (Yale) serve as a prototypical example. Watkins has a really lovely voice—flexible, strong, and tender. And he captures throughout his readings the supple, sensitive rhythms for which his poems are remarkable. But in only two poems on his Yale record, the first and last—both of them narrative ballads—do we hear fully the rich dramatic play of his verse. Where the voice becomes more personal, as it does in all the other poems he recorded for Yale—where the "I" of the poem is more plainly related directly to the poet himself—Watkins permits himself to be driven so hard by rhythmic beat that it muffles the emotions of the poem, and his rendering of the voice within the poem becomes imprecise.

Watkins' case is characteristic (I cite him because his readings are, withal, commanding) in its emphasis on expressing rhythmic surge at the expense of attitude, or drama. Probably there is one overwhelming reason for this partial achievement by many, perhaps most, poets—the poet can tuck into it snugly without risking personal exposure. The semantic or attitude-complex, the dramatic dimension, of the poem is more demanding and more dangerous. Giving into it totally the poet can lose not only his senses but, worse, the beat.

It is interesting to note that the famous professor, I. A. Richards, is one of the best of the recorded readers, teasing the drama out of his meters (Library of Congress). Before Richards' poetry one has a choice. I myself take the view that it really is poetry and not just criticism off on a lark. But Richards is too sizeable a critic, and too lately come to poetry, to be identified as a poet for at least a couple of generations. Thus his skill in oral reading—based, we must think, on his years of experience as a teacher and public lecturer—stresses its distinction as an art from the art of poetry.

Of course numerous recorded poets other than Richards read with a keen sense of attitude. On the R. P. Blackmur album (Yale), for example, his reading is referred to, through quotation from one of his own poems, as a "kind of violence in gear." It is a just suggestion of the poet's dramatic presence, though we may feel more gear than violence.

Let us conclude this brief chapter, intended only to suggest some values in listening to and studying poets' recordings of their works, in this way. Poets, reading aloud, provide rich hints which few other readers can give into important qualities of their poetry. Few poets, probably, recapture the full lives of the poems they have created. But theirs is still the power uniquely to return our attention to their works, and to contrast with their actual performances the ideal voices of their poems, as those poems may come to fulfillment in our imaginations.

6

DRAMATIC ANALYSIS
OF LITERATURE

Doubtless more than one order of analysis may reveal one or another aspect of a richly organized work of literary art. As I. A. Richards puts it, "Language — and pre-eminently language as it is used in poetry — has not one but several tasks to perform," and again, "The all-important fact for the study of literature . . . is that there are several kinds of meaning."[1] For the oral interpreter, seeking to express or suggest attitude and action precisely, surely one of the most valuable analytical approaches is based on the view of literature, lyric poems as well as plays, as a dramatic use of language.

This view is rooted in the understanding of literature as a representation of selected experience. *Experience* here means what we ordinarily mean by the term: the feelings, responses, and evaluations which are generated by and encompass various situations. For example, a man irritated by a dog's barking, says angrily, "That damned dog," leaves him and forgets him; and this has been his experience of the dog. Our experiences in life can be seen as a series of situation-attitude relationships. We may trace out these situations and attitudes by discovering the dramatic elements of the experience, i.e., by finding answers to the following questions: Who is performing What action of thought or feeling or deed? Where, when, how, and why performed? Summary answers to these questions, for instance, traditionally provide the news-

1. I. A. Richards, *Practical Criticism* (New York: Harcourt, Brace & Company, 1950), p. 180.

paper man reporting on one human event or another with the first paragraph of his story.

Literature, a representation of experience, can be approached the same way. In finding answers to these questions—Who? What? How? Where? When? and Why?—we are discovering the situation-attitude relationships which comprise the piece's "drama." In order to understand a piece, doubtless we need not always know the answers to all of these questions. But frequently enough our analysis and understanding of a given piece may become more secure when we discover in the work answers to these questions and to a seventh: how do the answers to who, what, why, etc., relate to one another?

By way of illustration, let us turn to a specific poem, "Loveliest of Trees," by A. E. Housman. The approach to it, by way of dramatic analysis, is obviously also frequently adaptable to the analysis of still more difficult poems and other forms of literature.

> Loveliest of trees, the cherry now
> Is hung with bloom along the bough,
> And stands about the woodland ride
> Wearing white for Eastertide.
>
> Now, of my threescore years and ten,
> Twenty will not come again,
> And take from seventy springs a score,
> It only leaves me fifty more.
>
> And since to look at things in bloom
> Fifty springs are little room,
> About the woodlands I will go
> To see the cherry hung with snow.[2]

In the perspective of dramatic analysis, the poem of course

2. From "A Shropshire Lad," Authorized Edition, from *Complete Poems* by A. E. Housman. Copyright © 1959 by Holt, Rinehart and Winston, Inc. Reprinted by permission of Holt, Rinehart and Winston, Inc., New York, Jonathan Cape, Ltd., and The Society of Authors, London.

may be seen as an act of the author himself. Kenneth Burke, particularly, has shown the values for literary analysis of such an emphasis, showing, for example, how much the full detail of "Samson Agonistes" is Milton's symbolic expression of reactions to his own situation in life.[3] Here, however, I am not thinking of the poem as the author's response to his own situation, valuable though such analysis might be in some other connection, but to the experience represented *in* the poem. Our interest will be in the reaction of the young man in, the "speaker" of, the poem to his situation as it is represented in the poem.

With respect to this poem, then, we may make rapidly six observations bearing on analysis of the poem's dramatic nature.

First, the dramatic elements of the experience represented can be discovered in answers to our six questions. (Who) A young man (Where) in the woods (When) in the spring (What) looks at cherry trees (How) with a keen awareness of their beauty (Why) because he is aware of the short time he has in life to look at beautiful things.

Second, these elements are organically related. Answers to "what" and "how" roughly give us the attitude: that is, (what) *looks* at cherry trees (how) with a keen awareness of their beauty. But the answer to the question "why" here becomes a link between attitude and situation, participating in both. But the situation itself—which we derive roughly from finding answers to Who? Where? and When?—also exerts a qualifying effect on the attitude. If, for example, the young man is looking at cherry trees (where) in an arboretum in the city, the poem is going to mean something subtly different; and if it is (who) a young bee wandering among the blossoms, the meaning is substantially altered. To notice this continual qualification of attitude by elements of situation is to see that an attitude is generated by and encompasses a situation.

Third, we should observe that our statement of these elements and their relationship to one another is not equivalent to what the poem says. For example, our suggestion that the attitude is one of "keen awareness" is obviously over-

3. Kenneth Burke, *A Rhetoric of Motives* (New York: Prentice-Hall, Inc., 1950), pp. 3-7.

simplified. It bears about the same relationship to the attitude that the word *democratic* does to some political act. Just as with the admittedly abstract word *democratic,* so does our phrase permit of many subscripts of substantially different significance: as, for example, it would be one thing to respond with "keen awareness" to the minister's decision to pass the collection plate twice and quite another to respond with "keen awareness" on finding Frankenstein had come to your birthday party. One must finally maintain that, though we might do better than the term *keen awareness,* the only way we could get the exact attitude, or meaning, would be to repeat the words in their order in the poem.

Fourth, it follows that when we discover a complication in the language of the poem we are also discovering new aspects or dimensions of attitude. For example, in this poem the young man's referring to his life expectancy as "seventy springs" is significant. It suggests that his is the interest of "spring," the interest in youthfulness in a green, blooming world. This suggests a special poignancy in his awareness of the cherry trees. Also we note that the rime and rhythm carry along the melancholy sense so firmly and briskly that we might term the rhythm *sprightly* or even *jaunty.*

This sense of rhythm leads us to a fifth consideration. A change in our understanding of one element in the situation-attitude relationship inevitably causes a change in our understanding of other elements. To notice the jaunty rhythm here may cause us to recall that (who) the young man is, after all, "only" twenty years old. Therefore, we may conclude that this has bearing on the "what" and "why" elements: maybe the young man, partly motivated by his awareness of life's shortness, is also inevitably motivated by his own youthful vigor. Then we should find his particular "keen awareness" taking the form of a delicious melancholy, a kind of adolescent joy in *Weltschmerz.* Certainly an analysis something like this of the interrelationship of "who," "what," and "why" factors causes some persons to discover something "humorous" in the poem. Others, able to see fifty years dashing off like fifty moments, see nothing at all humorous. Possibly the poem's most sympathetic reader will credit both qualities: it *is* humorous that a young man thinks how sad it is that he has only fifty years of life remaining, and it *is* just as sad as he thinks it is!

We may well have been brought by our dramatic analysis to consider a truly obscure aspect of this simple poem, an obscurity which, if we cannot neatly resolve, we can nevertheless profitably meditate. Doubtless dramatic analysis will not easily lead us to automatic illumination of obscure passages in poems, but frequently it will help us identify the source of obscurity and suggest whether or not the obscurity is some simple blemish in the poem, or a source of rich complexity of meaning.

The sixth thing we should notice in our dramatic analysis is that the young man's particular melancholy, delicious or otherwise, may so impress us that it appears to inform the "theme" of the poem: we may call it a poem in which a young man becomes aware of the shortness of life.

We are rather widely agreed today that the theme or "basic idea" of a piece of literature is but an aspect of its "total meaning." Some critics, it would seem, tend to regard themes, or ideas, or propositions about life as little more than points of departure for creating works whose values are largely formal. The excellent contemporary poet, Richard Wilbur, for example, once suggested that "I've thought of the poem as 'a box to be opened,' a created object, an altar-cloth, Japanese garden, or ship of death. Not a message or confession."[4] Such a statement vividly emphasizes how much interest may attach to structural aspects of the well-made serious work of literary art.

Nevertheless, as the poem orders its objects and emotions about, and even as its structural apologist protests its absolute innocence, we think the poem dreams to march on reality. It would seem that, however intricate or precious its being, even the poem that would most like to keep to its own company cannot resist poking into the world's business. Every now and then, even in the calloused modern world, we erect a Censor in praise of poetry's power, guessing its danger to us:

4. Richard Wilbur, "Commentary," Symposium on Richard Wilbur, *Berkeley Review 3* (1958), 49.

Did that play of mine send out
Certain men the English shot?[5]

Not even the Symbolists totally escaped making an impression. When Narcissus looks steadfastly away from men toward the water, someone else in this hustling world will always be there looking over his shoulder, to draw a conclusion, point a moral, expound a theme. And the toughest-minded aesthete has hard sledding to convince us that we should forego the thrill of recognition when, reading the poem, we read more deeply into the mystery of our own lives—even though ours should be like those profound discoveries made in sleep which we cannot quite remember when, rubbing the text from our eyes, we see again only the burly confusions of reality.

Dramatic analysis of literature offers us, as it relates to many or even to most poems and other literary forms, a way out of the impasse deriving from, on the one hand, the unacceptable view that a poem is merely an "illustration" of a theme or a basic idea and from, on the other hand, the view that ideas in a poem are merely insignificant aspects. In the dramatic perspective, thematic meaning is simply an inherent aspect of the whole experience represented in the poem.

"Meaning" is inseparable from represented experience in works of literature as it is inseparable from experience in life itself. Take for our homely example Aunt Matilda paying her relatives a visit. Her nephew greets her squirting his water gun at her and clutching her dress with jam-covered paws. "What an unruly little boy," thinks Aunt Matilda. The squirting water and smeared jam are particular enough, the unruliness is Aunt Matilda's idea. Maybe she is right and even the loving mother will think so, too. If so, the poor boy's judges would insist that their idea was a meaning riding in the jam-and-water, a meaningful and necessary implication of his action.

That is how much of the poem—a complex of images, acting and interacting—comes to us, not always firing water and

5. From William Butler Yeats, "The Man and the Echo," *Collected Poems of W. B. Yeats* (1959). Reprinted by permission of The Macmillan Company, New York, The Macmillan Company of Canada Ltd., Toronto, and Mrs. W. B. Yeats.

smearing jam, but, like the busy nephew, a bundle of particularities, a vibrant block of thinginess, a drama of interacting things and beings in their qualities.

We guess, then, that when we ask for the meaning of the poem, or of the play or story, we are often asking pretty much the same kind of question we ask when we ask what kind of boy is nephew Johnny. Meaning, as delivered by the critic who will risk handling its burden, is of an order comparable to that saucy substance we receive from Aunt Matilda when she tells us, too often even before we ask her, what kind of boy Johnny is, what a bundle of thinginess like that *means*.

Nor need we worry too much whether or not Aunt Matilda is absolutely right in her ideas about the action enveloping her. In the fast boil of human discussion, errors in critical analysis of meanings implicit in a being, whether the being is Johnny or the latest sonnet, have a way of evaporating, if only under the pressure of still fiercer errors. If our reading, whether of Johnny or the sonnet, is wrong, there will be some other Aunt Matilda around to set us straight.

It is our faith that a reading may be wrong. But we do well to have left over some faith in a variety of right readings. How shall we tell the most certain discovery of a work's themes and ideas from those discoveries not quite so good? Let us think that the finest reading makes itself known like a beauty queen, something standing out in the difference of opinion. It will not matter to the poem that means to mean which of its readers get first prize for judging. But such a poem needs the company of good hardy readers convinced that they have the right to look for, whether or not they prove of strength to find, meaning implicated in the forms of action.

When we consider meaning to be those significances, or revelations, arising from the action or experience represented in the piece, we see that meanings attach not only to the experience-as-a-whole but to various aspects of it. We may see not only all-embracing themes or propositions but meanings attaching to pieces of the action. We may note, for example, a comment on David Garrick's acting by Thomas Sheridan. Sheridan, an actor and one of the great English elocutionists who have greatly affected theory and practice of oral interpretation, was habitually alert to the full dramatic life of the imaginative worlds projected by words. So, in speaking of what he takes to be Garrick's failure to perform properly the role of Henry IV in the death-bed scene (Part II, Act IV, Scene 5), Sheridan attends to meaningful implications of a small portion of the action of the whole play: "Now Mr. Garrick in that famous scene whines most piteously when he ought to upbraid. Shakespeare has discovered there a most intimate knowledge of human nature. He shows you the King worn out with sickness and so weak that he faints. He had usurped the crown by the force of arms and was convinced that it must be held with spirit. He saw his son given up to low debauchery. He was anxious and vexed to think of the anarchy that would ensue at his death. Upon discovering that the Prince had taken the crown from his pillow, and concluding him desirous of his death, he is fired with rage. He starts up. He cries, 'Go chide him hither!' His anger animates him so much that he throws aside his distemper. Nature furnishes all her strength for one last effort. He is for a moment renewed. He is for a moment the spirited Henry the Fourth. He upbraids him with bitter sarcasm and bold figures. And then what a beautiful variety is there, when, upon young Harry's contrition, he falls on his neck and melts into parental tenderness."[6]

Obviously Sheridan is commenting on more than one aspect of the art of this scene, but among the things he wishes to note is Shakespeare's "most intimate knowledge of human nature," revealed by the full experience represented in the scene. That is, by his organization of materials Shakespeare gives us insight into "human nature." Probably when we speak of "meaning" in a piece of literature we mean primarily that the literary artist has communicated to us, has made possible, "insight"—insight into character, into relations between characters, into countless aspects of human experience. He has revealed to us, when we praise him for the meaningfulness of a part or of the whole of his work, a significance.

While the insights may attach to a small scene in a play or story, to a single metaphor or even a rhythmic shift in a

6. *Boswell's London Journal*, ed. Frederick A. Pottle (New York: New American Library, A Signet Book, 1956), pp. 134-135.

poem, we are of course particularly interested in that meaning, that "theme" or "basic idea," that big overarching meaning of the piece to which all the little, or lesser, meanings relate and from which the big meaning derives. We sometimes hear it said that the theme is, finally, the point of the poem. This way of looking is so natural, in fact, that even Professors Brooks and Warren, committed to the view of literature as dramatic discourse and strongly resisting the view which sees the piece as an illustration of the theme, nevertheless refer to themes as the "point" or "meaning" of the piece, putting the words in quotation marks to indicate their scruples.[7] But, to consider once more the little poem, "Loveliest of Trees," can we say that "the shortness of life" is, even in quotation marks, the point or meaning of the poem? That may well not appeal to all good readers as the final "point" of the poem: someone perhaps reliably sees the theme as the "inevitable sentimental sorrow of an adolescent," or another good reader sees it as "the saddening beauty of nature."

Perhaps we are on our way through theoretical difficulties of this sort when we recall once more that literature is a representation of experience. In life, a given experience probably cannot *mean* everything, but it can mean a number of things, and so, too, must we consider the relation of meaning to experience in literary representations. A poem like "Loveliest of Trees" conceivably has several "themes," and if we choose one we may do so because it seems overwhelmingly important, or perhaps we choose it merely for its convenient satisfaction of some immediate critical purpose of our own.

However that may be, the poem should not be taken as an illustration of meaning merely; it affords a new perspective and adds a new dimension. The "awareness of the shortness of life" is meaningful only insofar as that awareness has occurred in various persons in various situations, and every new awareness adds a fresh increment of meaning to that body of experience.

This new awareness, or new perspective on the "theme (s)," and not the theme itself is, if anything can properly be so

7. Cleanth Brooks and Robert Penn Warren, eds., *Understanding Fiction* (New York: F. S. Crofts & Company, 1943), p. 608.

called, the "point" of the poem. Since this new perspective develops only out of the context of the whole poem, all we can say accurately is that the point of the poem is the poem. Our analysis of dramatic elements may help us come closer to that broadly conceived "point." But we may think that a masterful oral reading, perhaps more fully than any other single act of elucidation, can communicate that "point" in all its roundness.

We may well ask further what is the relation of the theme or themes, the idea or ideas of the piece of literature, to life itself? In what sense is the ideational content of a piece *true?* It would be true, we should suppose, in the sense that it is true of the pattern of particulars dramatically organized within the piece. We may think, for example, of certain critics who have suggested that the central idea of Richard Wright's *Native Son* is the truth-claim that the only freedom remaining to modern man is the freedom to destroy, first others and finally himself. Put more accurately, perhaps, we would say that this idea is true of the world, the pattern of experience, created in *Native Son,* and that, to the extent the pattern of particulars in *Native Son* is a reflection of (or congruent to) the pattern of particulars in the world of raw experience, the idea will also be true of the "real" world. Put shortly, what is true of experience presented in *Native Son* will tend to be true of those aspects, if any, of life experience which resemble it.

The oral interpreter, as oral interpreter, has no more than any other student to say about the reliability of connections between literature and the life it represents. But in bringing the work vividly before our minds and imaginations, the proficient oral interpreter contributes his good share to our making the connections possible.

7

NOTE ON MATERIALS

FOR READING ALOUD

We have been discussing some aspects of analysis of literary texts. There is a further question concerning selection of the texts to analyze and to read aloud. It may be reasonably urged that some works *must* be read aloud if anything like their full appreciation is to be realized — early ballads, for example, designed for interaction between a public reader and the chanting chorus of his audience. Sometimes this reasonable view may slide off into an imposition of overly narrow limits on oral interpretation. It is then said, or implied, that the only works which *should* be read aloud are those limited to broad, simple, easily perceived effects: Boomalay, boomalay, boom!

Obviously in the perspective followed in this book any work of literature that can be read silently *may* also be read aloud. Whether or not it can be read aloud profitably will depend on numerous factors of a specific situation. The student reading aloud, or *sotto voce,* to improve his understanding of a text enjoys a simple situation which handsomely provides for his tackling the most intricate or difficult piece. He may well decide to deliver that piece to an audience, but then he will have to think hard concerning what he will say *about* the piece in order to make his expression of it available to his listeners. But there is no need for us to consider here all the things one should think about before deciding to read a given poem to an audience, so long as it is understood that the special value claimed for oral interpretation in this book is that it contributes to an understanding of truly good literature, literature that is always seriously fashioned and is frequently complex in structure and effects.

Consider the probable materials in a couple of college courses in oral interpretation. I point to a fairly usual situation in which an introductory course in the subject will be followed by at least one advanced course. For the introductory course the students will probably read from one or another of the many good anthologies of poetry or fiction, or both, from the kind of anthology he would read in an early college course in literature. The instructor may well select and assign the pieces to be read. If he does so it will probably be because he wishes the class as a whole to consider some pattern of literary and interpretation problems emerging from his selections. In the advanced course in oral interpretation, the instructor might well aim at helping his students to a partial mastery, at least, of some given poet—Hardy, let us say, or Yeats or Donne—or of some given fictionist of major stature, with each student eventually presenting a lecture-recital of the writer's work.

This is a mere adumbration of possibilities, for I do not mean to recommend a specific program; that can only be done satisfactorily within a given situation. But the examples mentioned at least suggest the proper line of direction for the student of oral interpretation of literature. He cannot expect a total knowledge of literature from his work in oral interpretation. What he can expect is a new kind of acquaintance with the same order of literature that he studies elsewhere.

There is a level of discussion at which we are right to guard against becoming arrogant in discussing literary value. The English professor is up against it just as we are in trying to decide whether or not Shelley should go up the scale and Donne down or vice versa, or whether Archibald MacLeish is in the canon or out of it. What he is up against are the most intricate value-problems and the most subtle value-theories.

But at the practical level of drawing up college reading lists, the problem really disappears. Or, to put it another way, it should appear for the teacher of oral interpretation in no more sinister form than it appears for the teacher of English.

72

Each teacher is committed to the presentation of works of such-and-such qualities, much as an American jurist is, I suppose, confined to the elucidation of a certain order of law. That is, each teacher assumes the burden of a slowly developing and slowly changing canon of "good" literature, from which he must select according to his and his colleagues' evaluations and the extent of the program in which he participates.

The really necessary work, then, for the teacher of the oral interpretation of literature is not to slay the ultimate dragons of value-theory; it is, more simply, to make a proper selection for study in oral interpretation from the kind of literature traditionally offered within the liberal arts program.

It is thought by some persons that to restrict the oral interpretation student's reading fare to truly good or serious literature is to tyrannize over his natural tastes. It is better for the student, according to this argument, to read Robert Service with gusto than to read William Butler Yeats in a daze. But this is to place the student's problem, and his opportunity, in a false perspective. He does not need to be a student in order to enjoy and understand Service, for he does that already. He is a *student* because he wants—he has the obligation to want!—to *learn* how to stop reading Yeats in a daze. And the instructor does not wish to confirm his students in their natural tastes; he wishes to help them improve their sense of what it is natural to like. He does not tyrannize over natural tastes, he civilizes them.

Thus we would agree fully with the view expressed by Donald Hargis that "when the interpreter chooses his materials to read aloud he must not only understand their meaning, but he must also sympathize with these ideas, enjoy them, and agree with them, in order to communicate the thought which the author intends."[1] But we should be careful to understand that this does not mean that the student should read aloud only what requires of him no study or imaginative effort to understand. To believe that would be to assume something that no teacher dares to accept: that the student's mind is a closed corporation of evaluations, opinions, and prejudices,

1. Donald Hargis, "What Is Oral Interpretation?" *Western Speech*, XVI (1952), 178.

which no widening familiarity with great literature under the guidance of sympathetic instruction can extend. There is a sophistic view of oral reading as there is of public speaking, according to which the instructor says to his student, "Say to me or read to me what you like; I will comment on your melody pattern."

The reader, then, must understand and sympathize with the materials he reads in order to do a good job of oral reading. But that may well mean — let us, if we are students or teachers, hope that it will mean — that he must stretch himself to understand and sympathize. Not only in prison is it sometimes humanly valuable for the person to do a long stretch! Finally, to notice the reader's need for understanding and sympathy is simply to become fully aware of the demands placed on both teachers and students of oral interpretation.

The teacher must obviously be competent to aid his students in the understanding of literature — the literature of the great fictionists and the great poets. Patently, it will not be sufficient for the teacher of oral interpretation to scan the curriculum of the English department and then piously introduce this "accepted" literature into his own course. What is demanded of him is not piety but awareness. He must know how language works in literature and be competent to elucidate the patterns of the best works. He must be the kind of instructor who can aid his students in such tasks as understanding by comparison and contrast the function of allusion in Milton and the function of allusion in Eliot; he must be able to notice and distinguish the kinds of symbolism in Melville and Kafka; he must understand and be able to teach understanding of all elements of a story or a poem in their organic relationships. He must know these things because, according to the familiar dictum, he must know the art if he is to express it — and because the art of serious literature, rich treasure that it is, does not easily become the possession of any man. The instructor may hope to delight his students with the rewards of close study, but that close study must be obtained.

The student's obligation, then, is to make the intellectual effort required to understand the selection with which he is confronted and the imaginative effort to sympathize with its contents. That is, simply, his obligation is to think of himself as the college treats him, as an educable human being.

Such an attitude, desirable in all of the student's work, is especially so in his relationship to literature; it requires nothing more than a proper observation of the nature and value of literature. Whatever else they may be, works of literature are certainly "imaginative prehensions of the world,"[2] and they require of us — indeed, this is their virtue — that we see many aspects of our world in a light which would otherwise be unfamiliar or unknown to us. In Coleridge's brilliant phrase, the reader must exercise "that willing suspension of disbelief for the moment, which constitutes poetic faith."[3] This is not a mere coaching in relativism; it is an extension of the borders of thought and human sympathy. That person who is least secure outside the confines of his own opinions and beliefs, who cannot hear contradictory opinions in the realm of politics or religion, for example, without experiencing the most disturbing emotions, may nevertheless find it possible to appreciate the insights of literature despite any disturbing implications. Yvor Winters, for example, perhaps the best-known modern absolutistic critic, puts this clearly in his remarks on Wallace Stevens' poem, "Sunday Morning." Winters, approving the poem as "one of the few great poems of the twentieth century in America," suggests that its doctrine is essentially "Paterian hedonism." Winters then indicates that his "dislike for the philosophy is profound"; yet he goes on to say, "But I know that hedonists exist, and the state of mind portrayed in the poem seems proper to them, and moreover it seems beautifully portrayed."[4] Manifold life and the manifold literature which represents it may ask at least this degree of tolerance from the most absolutistic observer.

If, in taking such an attitude, we properly appreciate the nature of literature, we are, incidentally, provided with one of our most powerful reasons for approaching it through oral

2. D. G. James, "I. A. Richards," *Critiques and Essays in Criticism, 1920-1948*, ed. Robert Wooster Stallman (New York: The Ronald Press Company, 1949), p. 472.
3. Samuel Taylor Coleridge, "From Biographia Literaria, XIV," *Essays in Modern Literary Criticism,* ed. Ray B. West, Jr. (New York: Rinehart & Company, Inc., 1952), p. 8.
4. Yvor Winters, *In Defense of Reason* (Denver: Alan Swallow, 1947), p. 476.

interpretation. When a student's study of literature is evaluated according to his ability to abstract from it its themes or to remember his instructor's opinions of it, he may possibly receive commendation for his study without ever having submitted his imagination to the whole of the work. But in an oral reading, if the student is to reproduce the attitudes and feelings of the work, he must obviously first experience them. The instructor's job is not one of telling the student to experience merely what the student likes or what he has already experienced; such advice would mark only an individual educator's despair. It is instead his job to help the student participate imaginatively in what he does not like or what is, in many particulars, foreign to his experience. This is to share in the task of the humanities to widen and enrich the individual experience.

It is sometimes urged that, apart from the question of the relation of the reader to his material, his selections of pieces for reading aloud should be dictated primarily by the nature of his audience. It is said that he must take into account the "interests, experience level, and capacity for understanding" of the audience.

To some extent, this maxim has little to do with oral interpretation of literature in the classroom situation. I presume that in such a situation the poem or story is usually read aloud only after the class as a whole has become somewhat familiar with it through private reading and class discussion. Such a procedure deprives the reader of a chance to stun his "audience" of fellow students with a surprise ending but, happily, little of the literature he reads in such a class will be limited to primitive qualities. Instead, for the oral reader in this situation, his reading will be the means of making public his own impression of and insight into the piece, and for his fellow students his reading will be a model for comparison with their own insights and impressions; while for the class as a whole, including the instructor, the reading will provide a concrete stimulus to other shared contemplations of a piece that deserves rereading.

But let us imagine a class in which all the members eventually present programs of readings before some group of persons other than their classmates: one of them will read for a literary club, another for a fraternity banquet, still another for a businessmen's luncheon group, etc. Obviously, given public-reading situations of this sort, the reader's program should be formed in accordance with an analysis of the nature of the audience. But to analyze an audience situation carefully does not mean that the oral interpreter should merely guess what selections his audience will be bound to like and then read them, regardless of those pieces' literary merit.

The oral reader in his public function has a different and greater responsibility. His responsibility is not to avoid reading serious literature to the "average" audience but to make serious literature *available* to the average audience.

To think that serious literature is actually "addressed" to somebody or to some particular mental and psychological limitations is, ordinarily, to commit the fallacy of confusing a piece of literature with a whisky advertisement. Even superior work which seems to "address" a particular audience — one recalls, for example, Pope's satires, the occasional poetry of Dryden, even some of the work of Shakespeare — is memorable, we think, because it was so well formed that it transcended its local purpose. Much of the worst of these — and other — writers' work is bad, we suppose, just because it was so particularly "addressed" to some particular audience. In our time, no one has been more insistent on the "communicative" aspects of literature than I. A. Richards, yet he concludes that, "Those artists and poets who can be suspected of close separate attention to the communicative aspect tend . . . to fall into a subordinate rank."[5] Richard Wilbur writes suggestively of this matter, "A poem is addressed to the Muse," and then he says explicitly that with which most serious writers would surely agree: "During the act of writing, the poem is an effort to express a knowledge imperfectly felt, to articulate relationships not quite seen, to make or discover some pattern in the world. It is a conflict with disorder, not a

5. I. A. Richards, *Principles of Literary Criticism* (New York: Harcourt, Brace & Company, 1925), p. 27.
6. Richard Wilbur, "The Genie in the Bottle," *Mid-Century American Poets,* ed. John Ciardi (New York: Twayne Publishers, 1950), pp. 2-3.

message from one person to another. Once the poem is written and published, however, it belongs to anyone who will take it, and the more the better."[6]

The oral interpreter's job, as public performer, is to make the good books sell better. He has two chief means of making the work available to audiences. One means depends on the most acute sort of audience analysis: he must learn what and how much he must say to a given audience in order properly to frame or introduce his material. Here all his means of persuasion and adaptability to audience limits are of utmost importance. But to make an audience pleased with the possibility of hearing a significant or great work is a very different thing from ingratiating one's self with an audience by reading something that's bound to be "popular" with them. No doubt there are excellent human motives for reading the merely "popular" to people who ask for it—it is a way of increasing one's income or of keeping busy, for example. But such motives, innocent as they may be, have nothing to do with the oral interpretation of literature nor with the proper responsibilities of the teacher or student of oral interpretation.

The second means for communicating the difficult or superior work to the "average" audience is, of course, the reading itself. We may assume that the responsible oral reader has himself had a keen insight into the work and is so skilled in his communication of that insight that his reading itself provides a means of audience prehension. In short, listening to a skillful oral reading is itself one means of discovering the qualities of a given work of literature. For example, for some years a very appreciative public of "average" citizens has applauded the oral readings of Charles Laughton who, if he did not always read the greatest literature, neither did he read the kind of pocketbook pabulum on which it is often assumed that the "average" man sustains the life of his mind.

A really skillful criticism provides one order of insight into the nature of a piece of literature; a really skillful oral reading provides another order of insight. We may hope for the time when the colleges will produce as many students of literature capable of effecting the latter order as they have already so plentifully produced students capable of the former.

8

ORAL INTERPRETATION AS

AN ART OF COMMUNICATION

Everyone knows what oral interpretation is until he begins to define it. Then it becomes tempting, as with the definition of other things, merely to say what it is not. It is most usual to say that oral interpretation is not acting. In an age of professional and departmental specialization this is a commendably pure tactic, but it involves certain risks. In proving that oral interpretation is not acting, one is in danger of showing that neither is oral interpretation anything else. The actor is a person who delivers a literary author's sentences out loud, delivers them to an audience, and tries to deliver them well. If an oral interpreter does not do these things, it may well be asked what function remains to him.

Nevertheless, it must be admitted that there are noticeable, if not absolute, differences between oral interpretation and acting. For example, actors usually have to memorize their lines whereas oral interpreters ordinarily read from the printed page. Still, we know that many interpreters practically memorize their material and, in Hollywood, they have discovered that at least a few actors are better armed if they read lines held on blackboards outside the range of the camera. Again, it may be said that an actor is a limited oral interpreter. The actor speaks sentences in plays only and, at that, he is restricted to the sentences uttered by one character, whereas the oral interpreter is at liberty to read all the sentences of all the characters in a play. Also, he may read sentences out loud from any other kind of literature.

Superficial distinctions of this sort, where they are not merely snobbish, are really too simple to be admitted by self-respecting scholars. Consequently, numerous writers have sought to find in the psychological relations of reader to material a decisive difference between acting and oral interpretation. That is, not the kind or extent of the material read aloud but the attitude taken toward the material is said to determine whether delivery, even of the same play, is oral interpretation or acting.

At first glance this kind of psychological distinction seems to provide a promising line of analysis, for it has — unlike some of the lines pursued in this matter — the great advantage of being somehow rooted in experience: a number of observers have noted a certain emotional detachment particularly obtaining to oral interpretation.

Now it is a commendable thing to observe accurately that in a number of successful oral interpretations there is an element of emotional detachment. But it does not automatically follow that therefore an oral interpreter *ought* to be somewhat detached when he reads sentences aloud.

Yet, this is a conclusion frequently recommended to us. Oral interpreters who favor this conclusion term the mystery of emotional detachment "aesthetic distance," and doubtless the phrase has a certain sonority. However, the phrase offers to the actor who is not hypnotized by it a sinister opportunity. He may suggest, on hearing an oral interpreter advised to maintain an "aesthetic distance" from his material, that when you read a sentence as if you mean it, you are an actor; but when you read it as if you mean *some* of it, you are an oral interpreter. We may fear that, as presently used, the term's usual value is to poor readers who can maintain that the dullness of their readings is merely the result of their having aesthetically forced the literary work to keep its distance.

Happily, a less invidious explanation of the interpreter's emotional detachment, which does not at the same time require its constant presence in a reading, is open to us if we will but consider the different effects of the physical contexts of acting and oral interpretation. We may put the most important aspect of these different effects briefly: the physical context

80

of an actor's oral delivery *encourages* an identification between the interpreter's attitudes and those of the depicted character; whereas, the usual conditions of an oral interpretation *discourage* an identification between the attitudes of the interpreter and the character.

The conditions of an actor's oral delivery — his being assigned sentences of a single character, the assembly of other persons for other roles, and costuming, scenery, and lighting — are designed to encourage him to produce the effect of being the character whose words he utters aloud. Some actors, perhaps most of them in modern times, attempt to produce this effect of identification primarily by trying to *feel like* the character whom they portray. Still others attempt to assume the reality of the character chiefly by clever technical imitation of human attributes appropriate to the character. But regardless of his means the actor tries to give the effect of being the character whom he portrays, and this is true not only of the times when he is speaking but, what must be a greater challenge to his cleverness, even in those moments in a play when he must be silent and listen to other actors talk.

It will be suggested by some persons that in recent times there have been attempts by actors at a kind of detachment from the characters whom they depict. In some experimental dramatic performances, actors will speak sentences not as if they were characters of the play but somehow as if they are pointing to another place, perhaps in the author's or spectator's imagination, where those characters have their existence. It is interesting to observe that such experiments in acting are ordinarily accomplished by a decreasing illusion of the reality of physical circumstance. Theatres will not be darkened, costumes may be omitted, and the stage will either be empty or lightly stocked with a few suggestive objects.

This begins to partake of the usual physical context of an oral interpretation. On his podium, if the interpreter has the use of a podium, there may be a lectern and a glass of water, but these are for him and not for his *Hairy Ape* or lyric poet, as the case might be. As to costuming, if his selections are mournful, he will wear his black suit; if they are merely sober, he may wear his brown. Furthermore, if he reads a play, he will take all the parts himself, and not even the most fantastic imagination in his audience will fail to recognize that he cannot be everybody at once.

Again, as with a description of the actor's circumstances, it will be noted that there are variations from the usual situation of oral interpretation. Some interpreters use costumes, stage scenery, etc. Accompanying such changes there is ordinarily an increase in the degree to which the interpreter gives the effect of being the character or characters whom he depicts.

One actor-interpreter on several occasions attempted to suggest, through detailed costume and make-up, being the *author* of the works he read, so that the interpreter's audiences heard stories roared through the beard of Charles Dickens. Dickens himself made so much money reading aloud that it is tempting indeed to emulate him in a dry time. Still, though it is a compliment of sorts to resurrect the character of an author, if literary historians are right about the lives of authors, it can frequently be accomplished only at some risk of insulting the moral standards of the audience.

Despite occasional variations, then, it is obvious that physical circumstances usually discourage a high degree of identification between the oral interpreter and the character or characters speaking in the piece of literature. It is a mistake, nevertheless, to conclude that the interpreter, discouraged though he may be, therefore ought not to try to reproduce to a high degree the tone or attitude of speakers or characters within a piece of literature.

As we have seen, perhaps at no time so much as in the modern period have literary critics stressed the common dramatic basis of all forms of imaginative literature. Dramatic poetry is of course a case of drama as well as of poetry. The story or novel also has its evident dramatic aspect: characters speak back and forth to one another, and when novelists break in on the scenes of their imagination, as they decreasingly do these days, it is nevertheless frequently enough as a kind of other character, expressing, directly or implicitly, all sorts of feelings and opinions about what is going on.

But we have noted, too, that lyric poetry is declared by

most modern critics to have a dramatic aspect. Perhaps we go too far in declaring poetry to be universally dramatic in its expression of so many separate points of view and complexes of attitude. We may observe a rather different intent in some modern poems, usually written under the Imagist or Objectivist influence. Some of these poems, though admirable, seem to represent the rather humanly indifferent perceptions which one might expect of a typewriter with 20-20 vision. But whatever the exceptions, if any, most of us today find it valuable to make a "dramatic" distinction between the *author* and the *speaker* of a poem, even of such evidently "personal" or apparently autobiographical accounts as "Dover Beach" or "Composed upon Westminster Bridge" or "Dulce et Decorum Est."

Now, as we have seen, what is importantly a complex of attitudes — or, if you will, tones or feelings or emotions — can hardly be accurately communicated by something different from themselves. We may, for example, imagine a passage of poetry in which the speaker is in a *rage*. Even this is much too general a description of anything that is likely to be expressed in a poem, for a speaker is never just in a rage, but always in some kind of particular rage, of a degree and quality determined by any number of things, including what he is raging against. However, though this is but a general description of an attitude which might possibly inhere in some passage, still it is close enough a description to suggest clearly that it will hardly be precisely represented by a show of *petty irritation*. Whether or not we attribute the difference to aesthetic distance or something else, it still must be said that rage has not been expressed or suggested.

The audience, then, apparently has the right to expect a job of acting from the interpreter. The term *acting* here plainly refers to the interpreter's having a high degree of empathic response to the attitudes of speakers within a piece of literature. That is, the audience presumably expects from the interpreter a communication of the piece, and if, as with literature, the piece is probably dramatic in nature, the audience should expect it to be dramatized. If the poem is a little drama, the interpreter should give it a little production.

From these considerations it would seem that the oral interpreter who would perform effectively must steer a miserable course between Scylla and Charybdis. If the piece itself declares the need for a high degree of congruence between its own attitudes, tones, and feelings, and those of any person seeking to communicate them, nevertheless everything in the interpreter's physical situation declares to the audience that he clearly is not the speaker or speakers whom he characterizes. He is seen to be, like themselves, a member of the audience for the selection which is being read.

But reference to Scylla and Charybdis, though classic, too simply images the difficulties of the interpreter, for in neither of his roles, as public performer or as another member of the author's audience, are his duties undivided.

As public performer, the interpreter is required not only to be an actor but also a public speaker. In whatever introductory or transitional material he utters—whether to elucidate, to praise, or to relate his selections to other works or to the interests of the audience—the interpreter becomes a public speaker, subject to the same general principles which govern any other attempt to inform, to persuade, and to argue. He is, even in those silent spaces between selections, a public speaker who will determine the length of his pause and what he does or says in it according to his sense (and it is a sense rather than a formula which operates) of what will best further audience understanding and appreciation. Doubtless, ideally the interpreter would not even drink water or scratch his head without considering the effect of such actions on the tensing or relaxing of audience interest, but we must recognize with these, as with other itches, human limitations.

It even frequently happens that during the course of the reading itself, the interpreter must attend to his role as public speaker. His tone or expression may, at some given moment, relate very loosely indeed to the material he reads, as he finds himself forced to account for some development affecting audience attention: for example, a number of late arrivals or, an even worse prospect, a number of early departures. Such examples point only to the more obvious causes of modifications in the interpreter's expression of a piece. Far more subtle causes operate, deriving both from the general nature of a given audience and from the interpreter's moment-by-moment relation with its members. His awareness of the psychological state, or condition, of his audience will — or ideally ought to — at all times affect the interpreter's expression of his material.

If his position as a public performer requires his sensitivity to states of mind, as another member of the author's audience the interpreter is in the trying position of having everybody else watch him. At least he hopes they are watching him, and this will have an effect on his behavior. He will pay some attention to reacting as a member of the author's audience might be expected to react.

For one thing he will respond critically. One of my college speech instructors insisted that there is good scientific evidence for the belief that the normal mind can attend to some six or seven times as much material as can normally be spoken to it in a given period. True or not, it was improbable enough a theory to be memorable! If true, it may be little more than a suggestion that no one normally says anything much. But also it may suggest that one person cannot only listen to another but, if he will only put six-sevenths of his mind to it, think about what is said.

Certainly we know that, even while he is responding in one part of his being to a literary or dramatic action, the reader or viewer in another is briskly making such businesslike remarks as, "Now, that's a stupid thing to say," or "A daring piece of business, that," or "Eighteen lines and nary a rime!"

In the oral interpreter's expression, attitudes like these — sometimes supplanting, more frequently merging with or qualifying attitudes taken toward the piece itself — will play their part. It may be the suggestion, "This is relatively unimportant," or even, "I know this passage is a little dull, but hang on, the fine stuff's coming," or even, exuberantly, "Now wasn't that splendid!"

The interpreter, as member of the author's audience, is not only critic but also sympathetic sharer. That is, he will sometimes express attitudes which are not attitudes of the speakers or characters within a piece, but the different attitudes of the audience which are caused by the literary action. A broad example would be the audience's moment of hilarity during the episode in which the pompous man exasperatedly picks himself up from the icy street on which he has slipped.

If the interpreter chooses to express the audience's hilarity rather than the character's exasperation, it may be in part an ingratiating tactic. For how could he claim to be a good fellow and yet refuse to join in merriment so intense and widespread? But there is also in this sharing of the audience's mood a most tactful compliment to the author which should warm his heart. For in refusing to suggest the pompous man in his downfall, the interpreter is saying implicitly to the audience in whose laughter he joins, "Notice: you are not laughing at *my* highly maneuverable face and voice; all of us are laughing because of the author's skill." This may also suggest that the interpreter, as critical witness, will not join in an audience mood, however hearty, which in his opinion the art of the relevant passage has not earned.

In both aspects of his membership in the author's audience, as critic and as sympathetic sharer, the interpreter's reactions will doubtless merge with his public speaking, or persuasive, function. He will respond with some gusto, his heightened reaction implying that, since he finds the piece worth attending (and if he does not, he should not read it), the rest of his audience can like it, too.

Oral interpretation, then, is an unformulable amalgam of acting, public speaking, critical reaction, and sympathetic sharing. Close observation of a number of oral interpretations should confirm this view.

In this recognition of the multiple aspects of an interpreter's activities lies some suggestions for clarifying a number of problems confronting the student of oral interpretation.

First, it implies that it is desirable for the interpreter to have a high degree of empathic response to attitudes or speeches within the piece, for proper communication of dramatic material requires it. Take, for example, the passage in Wilfred Owen's "Dulce et Decorum Est" in which the speaker recalls a soldier caught unprepared by gas-shells:

But someone still was yelling out and stumbling
And floundering like a man in fire or lime. —
Dim through the misty panes and thick green light,
As under a green sea, I saw him drowning.

In all my dreams before my helpless sight
He plunges at me, guttering, choking, drowning.[1]

The interpreter should express the speaker's attitude of helpless horror toward this appalling vision and, if he can also manage it, perhaps something of the gassed soldier's own agony. The interpreter should express these things because they are fundamental aspects of the passage which it is his function to communicate.

Second, recognition of the interpreter's multiple activities permits us to note more accurately the causes and nature of limitations on the interpreter's empathic response to the attitudes of speakers within a literary piece. We need not fall prey to the hint that for some more or less mystic reason, each line must be read with a certain detachment. Instead, long passages or even whole poems may be read as if there were no distance at all between the attitudes of the interpreter and those of characters within the selection. Again, as the interpreter finds it necessary or appropriate to attend to his role as public speaker, critic, or sympathetic sharer, the distance between interpreter and literary speaker may widen slightly, or grow very great. We cannot, for example, say that the cited passage from Owen *must* be read with a high degree of empathic response. It should, if possible, because horror of a certain sort is the attitude which the passage seeks to communicate. But if some other aspect of his situation requires it, the interpreter's empathic response must be modified.

We may, if we wish, continue to speak of "aesthetic distance," but we will now understand it more clearly as a necessity of the interpreter's total situation, having different causes, and, as a result, ordinarily obtaining to the reading of various passages in a variety of quality and degree.

1. Reprinted from *Poems of Wilfred Owen* by permission of the publishers, New Directions, New York, and Chatto and Windus, Ltd., London.

Lest it be thought that this view too much emphasizes factors causing aesthetic distance as regrettable necessities, we should note that they are regrettable only when one idealizes human nature and audience behavior. If our hearts were at all times open to each current of the human spirit, it would indeed be a pity and a crime to weaken that current by sending it out through the aesthetic distances. But our hearts are not open. They are clogged where they are not sealed off in their own affairs. Consequently, we may quite accurately regard those aspects of the interpreter's work which lead him away from a direct expression of a piece's attitudes into preparing an audience for their reception, as his laudable effort to make his audience humane and open-hearted.

Third, the present view of the interpreter's activities dismiss as irrelevant the frequent interdict, referring particularly to gesture of arm and hand, against bodily activity in oral interpretation.

For the number of persons who have seen gestures used successfully in oral interpretation, strictures against them are likely to appear merely comical—rather like an attempt to draw up a code of conduct for the Tea Ceremony. But the matter cannot be so simply dismissed. Since it has been frequently observed that bodily movement tends to increase in proportion to emotional involvement, its proscription derives from the notion that aesthetic distance is an omnipresent necessity in oral interpretation, and is negated only when that notion is shown to be largely false.

Also it can be empirically shown that oral interpreters generally do not make as many large bodily gestures as actors, for example, are likely to make. But this is not because there is anything inherently wrong in an interpreter's gesture. We have already seen the greater number of limitations on his empathic response to attitudes of speakers within a piece, and these limitations frequently work to suppress gesture. But gesture can be successfully used by interpreters, and the entire argument can be summed up in a convincing tautology: when the interpreter's gesture is successful, then it is successful.

Fourth, this view of his many-faceted function helps to verify the assumption that oral interpretation is an independent art.

This assumption is sometimes thought to be too embarrassing to accept as true. It suggests that the reader of disgraceful material may be an artist, whereas the reader of true literary art may be disgraceful.

As with other disagreeable facts, some students of interpretation have sought to explain this one out of existence. They suggest that oral interpretation is an art only when the material read is an art. But this is to confuse the nature of a thing with its impact. It is quite true that an excellent reading of a great poem will be more rewarding than an excellent reading of a poor poem, for that auditor prepared to understand both. It is also true that good material—that is, material with a certain density of effect—will possibly put greater demands on an interpreter's art than poor material. Yet this is certainly not always the case, as many a misled interpreter who has sweat to salvage a piece of literary junk can testify.

From considerations like those made above of the interpreter's activity, we must conclude that oral interpretation is an art independent of the nature of what is read. We have seen that oral interpretation is an unformulable amalgam of several activities. It is the oral interpreter's *art*—and it is in this sense that he is artist—to proportion this amalgam in a concrete situation.

If this is true, what are we to make of the oral interpreter's capacity to deliver well that which—in terms of literary quality—might better remain undelivered? Well, let us not criticize the art of interpretation, for to read poor literature aloud is, after all, a decision we need not make. Rather, let us, if we can sufficiently abstract ourselves from his material when it is impoverished, applaud the good public reader's art; for, in considering oral interpretation's bearing on literary study, we do well to recognize it as an independent art of some complexity.

This is not sufficiently understood. Many literary persons —among them perhaps those most zealous for the prosperity

of serious literature—fear if they do not disdain oral interpretation. They associate it with artifice and exhibitionism
and, in an effort to avoid these possible crimes by a speaker
against a cherished literary text, they assume that fully
understanding a truly good piece is enough to assure its
proper public reading.

Thus when these persons—frequently good scholars and
critics—address the pieces or passages they admire, to students or to other audiences, they read with such splendid
subjective appreciation, and also usually with such excellent
pronunciation, that they can scarcely believe that what is so
easy for them to do can be so ill-received. Often they may
blame their bored audiences for coarseness of sensibility,
and perhaps sometimes they are right. But frequently enough
they have themselves to blame for reading good work poorly—
either because they are without talent for public reading (and,
regrettable though it may be, that mysterious basic quality
is rather more of a gift than an achievement) or because they
are untrained and inexperienced in the art of public delivery.
It is well that they understand the difficulties of that art
before they practice it.

In this chapter and those preceding, we have suggested
that the oral interpreter should know how literature works,
and what its elements are, that he should be able to bring
this knowledge to bear on particular works of literary art,
and that he should be able to communicate vividly to an audience his own achieved awareness of specific works.

This is to say that it is the task of the interpreter, highly
aware of a given piece of literature, to affect the auditor's
awareness of the piece. The effect may be of various sorts. It
may sometimes be almost a direct transference, so that the
high degree of the interpreter's awareness becomes the
auditor's own. More often, it may be a correction or extension
of awareness, as when someone already familiar with a poem
has some further facet of it revealed to him by another person's
public reading of it. It may be an encouragement to awareness, as when someone is motivated by a public reading to
study some poem of which an oral interpretation made him
more or less vaguely aware. But, whatever the specific result,

the oral interpreter of literature will seek to affect the auditor's awareness of the piece which is interpreted.

When the piece is good, when the interpreter intensely understands and vividly impresses it on the minds of his auditors, we may say that his art of communication serves literature well.

9

THE EXPRESSION OF
THE ORAL INTERPRETER

In the previous chapter, in considering oral interpretation as a speech art, we viewed it as an art of *communication*. We saw that the interpreter, in communicating a text, must take account of his relationship both to the text and to the audience, of which he is himself, in a certain sense, a member. We saw further that in order to communicate a written work the interpreter performs a multiple role as public speaker, actor, critical commentator, and sympathetic sharer.

In using the term *actor* I was thinking of that aspect of the interpreter's communicative art concerned with expressing what is orally expressible in a given text. To name three other aspects of oral interpretation does not mean that expressing the text is but one-fourth of the interpreter's job. It is, rather, so obviously of central importance that some persons take it for the whole of the art.

Consequently, let us move in for a closer look at the interpreter's expression of a text. We shall here think of all his other roles as merely so many means by which he keeps his audience alert to the text he is reading, and concern ourselves solely with those elements of a text which the interpreter can express, the value of his expression of them, and the means by which he expresses them.

One can of course describe what is expressible in a text at different levels of generality. Perhaps the most general description possible would suggest that the interpreter can express the qualities and the relative importance of linguistic elements of a text. We know, for example, that some words in a sentence are more important than others in conveying meaning, that some sentences in a paragraph carry more weight than still other sentences, that some passages in a text are more crucial than others. To communicate a text publicly we must preserve these hierarchies of significance as they appear in the text. Keeping to an hierarchical figure, perhaps we should say that the interpreter should *respect* the orders of importance, because that implies a nicety of discrimination which is necessary for the good reading aloud of any text. One cannot merely divide that throng of linguistic elements into a few groups—the *loud,* the *soft,* the *fast,* and the *slow,* for example—and then, as it were, seat his groups indifferently in so many corners of a room. Rather, he must preserve the most careful court etiquette, knowing not merely that the barons must both bow first to the viscount, but also which baron has the right to pick up his fork first.

Although we may laugh a little at this Connecticut Yankee's Court of Discourse, it is nevertheless worth mentioning to indicate the particular attention which the oral interpreter must give all the words and elements of his text, in their complicated relations to one another; and it is, perhaps, as satisfactory a general description of what an oral interpreter can express as any other.

Here, however, let us consider what the oral interpreter can express in terms of aspects of experience, real or imagined, which the elements of a text may evoke. A less general order of description, it is better adapted to the literary text, which is our present chief concern.

Put simply, the oral interpreter can express attitudes, properties of objects, and actions.

From our preceding discussions, you will understand that by *attitudes* we mean that the interpreter can express an author's or his fictive characters' "sadness," "happiness," "jocularity," and such qualities, in their various modulations and levels of intensity. Such qualities are often referred to as "emotions" or "feelings," which are also adequate names for them.

If we ordinarily prefer to think of these qualities as "attitudes," it may be because the word better suggests cognitive elements. We may think of *emotion* as something detached from contemplation of a stimulus. A person may, for example, feel considerable emotion when he burns his fingers on a hot stove, without paying much attention to the qualities of the stove. In literary texts, however, emotions are ordinarily related to an author's (or his characters') assessment of a situation, so that our hero's "sardonic humor" comes after much observation of the fool on whom he unleashes his wit, or another's "rage" develops as he *thinks about* disagreeable qualities in some object or person.

Doubtless interchanging words like "attitude," "emotion," "feeling," and even "tone" sometimes creates unfortunate ambiguities, but so long as we recognize that this is the case, we can usually figure out what a given writer is talking about in a given context. Perhaps we may best think of *attitude* as any state of mind (it may be that of the author or of his fictive character or characters) evoked by the text.

Properties of objects comprise the second class of elements which an interpreter may express.

Let us consider a phrase: "Gingerbread is preferable to hardtack." It is possible, as we have seen, for the oral reader to indicate *preference*—that is, to take an attitude toward "gingerbread" and "hardtack": a smile on uttering "gingerbread," a look of disdain, a sneer in the voice on uttering "hardtack." (You will be right to maintain a proper "skeptical poise" on hearing these descriptions.) But as well as taking an attitude, the reader may suggest (though unquestionably in "thin strokes" or, in Korzybski's useful metaphorical phrase, by a "high order" of abstraction) properties of the object. Perhaps the significant properties which could be suggested here would be properties of *texture* (the soft-ness of gingerbread, the hard-ness of hardtack): a soft, luxurious quality of voice, let us say, for "gingerbread," a clipped, shorter articulation of "hardtack."

Permit me at this point briefly to anticipate a discussion of the interpreter's means of expression, because the ability of the oral interpreter—himself an "object" of a special sort, a live human being—to suggest through his own activity properties of such objects as gingerbread and hardtack may seem initially much harder to understand than his ability to express the attitudes of speakers or "characters," human beings like himself. The interpreter has a number of methods, through effective physical movement and gesture, to suggest properties, but his vocal means are perhaps most easily described, and most important.

You will notice from the example above that a suggestion of properties is created by a kind of *auditory metaphor:* the texture of gingerbread relates to the texture of hardtack as the texture of one "noise" made by the interpreter relates to another. But let us leave our hardtack for a moment to turn to a line from an actual poem: "My love is like a red red rose." We may safely assume that the repetition of "red" suggests an especially vivid rose (that is, a rose whose property of color is an intense redness). This quality of intense or vivid color may possibly be suggested by a certain intensity of sound-effect. For example, the interpreter may create his sound-effect by an increase of his normal volume and a more than usual prolongation of the vowel as he reads the words "red red," and, furthermore, the quality of his pause between the first "red" and the second one will probably serve to link the words very closely, as if together they make one bright bright red.

There is no need to stress the obvious point that there is nothing inherent in *any* noise which will immediately evoke in a listener the notion of gingerbread or hardtack or a red red rose. Nor need we puzzle the troubling question of onomatopoeia: whether or not, for example, the sounds of "s," "f," and "z" make "sizzle" sizzle and "fizzle" fizzle. It is not really a matter which need greatly concern the oral interpreter (as performer, at least, if not as scholar). If something inherent in the sound of a word permits him to suggest, merely by uttering the sound, some property or quality of an object, well and good. By and large, however, he may assume that his own auditory metaphors—with which, as in the "intense" delivery of the vivid rose, he creates suggestions of properties—become meaningful only in the enunciation of verbal symbols, with specific denotations and fields of connotation.

Before leaving this matter of properties, we should note

that our discussion has concerned what the interpreter *may* express and not what he *must* express. It is rather hard, for example, to imagine that passage in the reading of which it would be *important* for the oral interpreter to distinguish the textures of gingerbread and hardtack; on the other hand, it is rather obviously important, in reading Burns's poem, to deliver up a vividly red rose. It may also be noted that, once the interpreter has determined that it is important to suggest the property of an object, it remains for him to consider how fully, or fleetingly, the text requires that he should "construct" the quality: he must learn from his full understanding of the text just *how* red is the rose. Decisions of this sort confront the interpreter phrase by phrase, word by word, "nay, letter by letter." But then, I am not trying to prove that his art, in its full development, is a simple one!

A suggestion of properties is, to be sure, so fused with attitudes taken toward objects that frequently they can hardly be separated, either in their production or effect. In the case of the vivid rose, for example, we may also find the interpreter delivering it to us *fresh* or *tender:* a quality of that sort might be involved if the interpreter renders the tenderness of the speaker's attitude in comparing his beloved to a new June rose. Still, the reader may prove the distinction made here quickly enough to his own satisfaction by twice reading the statement above concerning gingerbread and hardtack, once attempting to communicate some idea of *preference,* and again attempting to communicate a notion of preference for a *soft* object to a *hard* object (to suggest a preference for a *tasty* object would basically involve us in an expression of attitude: that is, we may know that gingerbread is *tasty* because of the attitude taken toward it, some variation of stomach-rubbing and lip-licking).

Alertness to the properties attributed to objects in a given text serves to discipline the interpreter's expression of attitudes. That is, only by his alertness to the qualities of objects toward which attitudes are taken by the author or his characters, can the interpreter express the correct *intensity* or level of attitude. Let us imagine that we do indeed hear an interpreter say, "Gingerbread is preferable to hardtack," with wide smiles, stomach-rubbings, and before he is through with the phrase, wide wide sneers and bitter growls. Something is rotten, this side of the gingerbread. Simply, we know what attitude to take, in its exact measure or intensity, because we know toward *what* the attitude is taken.

Actions of one sort or another comprise the third class of elements which the interpreter can express. We may relate this class to the previous one by saying that the interpreter can denote *dynamic* properties of persons, objects, or events. A good example of this might be found in the phrase of Arnold's where he talks of the sea's "melancholy, long, withdrawing roar," which the reader can express by suggesting in the context of briefer vocal signs, this "long" withdrawing-ness.

If it is thought that this example too much overlaps the above function, as an illustration of ways in which properties of objects may be suggested, a better example might be taken from Shakespeare:

How shall summer's honey breath hold out
Against the wreckful siege of battering days?

One effective way of expressing this line would be to suggest, among other things, the nature of the action. "Days" are compared to the relentless, inexorable battering-rams of a feudal siege, so in reading the line we could emphasize the regularity of meter until "battering," which could be, in effect, "vibrated" against "days." That is, it would be possible to suggest something of the slow, regular, methodical way in which the soldiers lift the heavy ram, swing it regularly back and forth, and smash it into the gate.

You will notice that these three expressible aspects of a text do not lie side by side, like sticks in a box, but grow into and out of one another, like fingers on a palm, and perhaps we could generalize their expressibility in this way: They are related elements of that literary experience evoked by the text, which the oral interpreter can translate to and express in his own behavior.

Now if literature is, as we have said, a representation of experience and if the interpreter precisely expresses this experience through his projection of attitude, action, and object, it would seem evident that he has accomplished something of importance in making a literary experience available to an audience. Naturally, his services may not be required. The attitudes, after all, are there, richly impregnating the literary text. His bloodshot eyes enthralled by his book, the solitary silent reader, someone will say, can get all these attitudes and all this experience for himself. So of course he may. He may get the attitudes in their exactness just as he may get everything else which criticism offers him by himself. What shall we care what the professor thinks of the unity of *War and Peace* if we have already thought of it ourselves? How can we be excited by the seven types of ambiguity if we have already found eight?

This kind of thinking does not imply that criticism is not valuable. It is only because we think it is, or can be, of considerable value that we can have the same faith in oral interpretation, as an order of insight into a work of literature. Critics, like oral interpreters, must base their claim to value on the assumption that all readers are not perfectly alert, and that even alert readers can learn things about a rich text from one another. The student working with a line in order to read it well aloud may at last discover the attitude which eluded him, first in his eye and mind, next in his voice. The expert critic may also learn something from the expert reading, like the teacher who accused Charles Laughton of cutting some of Shakespeare's passages to make them seem interesting. When Laughton showed that his reading had cut nothing, the English professor was pleased to confess that the oral reading had shown him the passage in a new light.[1]

This casting of new light is the basic job of all criticism, and when it comes to showing attitudes clearly, we may well think that the oral interpreter is the most suggestive and accurate of all critics. Of course we may always *write* our descriptions of the speaker's attitudes. We may say that he is jocular or happy or sad; we may bring to bear a modification or two, as when we say he is *wryly* humorous. But still we are

1. Charles Laughton, "Read It Out Loud," *This Week*, November 19, 1950, p. 7.

plagued—or ought to be plagued—by the question, "How wry? How humorous?" To discover that we must go back to the text and, at its best, oral interpretation can more effectively conduct us there, we may think, than any written comment.

Let us look at that literary text once more.

R. P. Blackmur, whose key critical term "gesture" is close to "attitude," writes of the matter in this way: "Gesture is not only native to language, it comes before it in a still richer sense, and must be, as it were, carried into it whenever the context is imaginative." Blackmur then shows concretely what he means by this. He tells of seeing a woman loaded down with packages trying to get to her seat in a moving bus, a woman who managed to express "by sniffs and snorts, by smiles, by sticking her tongue out very sharp, by batting her very blue eyes about, and generally by cocking her head this way and that . . . the whole mixed flourishing sense of her disconcertment, her discomfiture, her uncertainty." Blackmur concludes that "the highest use of language (that is, literature) cannot be made without incorporating some such quality of gesture within it."[2]

This view of literature can hardly fail to excite our interest in the potentialities of oral interpretation as a consequential aspect of literary study. If literature is constantly batting its very blue eyes about, so is the interpreter, whose sniffs, like literature's, must subtly relate and delicately harmonize with his snorts.

Surely, however humorously we put it, there is a strong suggestion in views like Blackmur's that an excellent way of understanding literature is to read it as teachers of oral interpretation emphasize that it must be read; that is, by appropriating to one's own organism the attitudes or gestures of a given piece—and by grasping the qualities of objects toward which the attitudes are taken.

The poet's business, we say, is to present imaginative worlds, bustling with attitudes, actions, and objects. Of course a poem is a meaningful world, but its meaning is immanent in the qualities which it presents. Without a grasp of those

2. R. P. Blackmur, "Language as Gesture," *Accent Anthology,* ed. Kerker Quinn and Charles Shattuck (New York: Harcourt, Brace & Company, 1946), pp. 468-469.

99

qualities—which through his devices of sound and imagery and connotation the poet seeks to evoke for us—we can hardly grasp the true meaning of his world, any more than in our coarse "real" world we could really understand the meaningful proposition that dogs are friends to man if we had never observed a dog or, at least, had it pretty well described to us.

An empathic response to these literary worlds, then, is not merely some talented trick of a good oral interpreter, but is also necessary, we think, to understand the particular kind of meaning which the literary structure can afford: that is, an experience which can literally only be understood when it is vicariously shared.

In pointing to the oral interpreter's empathic response to literature, we have begun to turn our attention to the means by which he expresses a text. To put it in the widest terms, he translates or "reproduces" the linguistic activity of the written scene into bodily activity.

But let us look at his means more closely, dividing his bodily activity into not-altogether arbitrary divisions so that we may discriminate more clearly its nature, and noting the ways in which he expresses attitudes, properties of objects, and actions. I shall suggest here three important means by which the interpreter expresses a text, though there are doubtless other ways, or at least other ways of looking.

We may note first that the interpreter expresses a text in facial, vocal, and bodily behavior.

In rendering a passage, a reader must often decide which of these three major expressive-areas should be emphasized. To say that the reader "decides" where his expressive emphasis shall lie does not mean that his is a necessarily conscious decision. As equally successful writers are quite differently "conscious" of their intentions, so, we may suspect, are equally successful interpreters. Nor do I mean, in referring to facial, vocal, and bodily areas, that an oral interpreter is a machine composed of three parts, like a fountain pen, holder, and scratch pad set. The oral interpreter is of course an organic being in whom all arbitrarily designated areas are affected simultaneously by emotion, so that facial, vocal, and bodily expression are nearly always interconnected. But, frequently

enough in a successful reading, there are meaningful variations in emphasis (during the reading of a word, or a phrase,
or the whole piece) on these expressive-areas.

Sometimes a given interpreter's commitment to one or
another of these areas is the result of personal limitations: a
reader who cannot convey much through facial expression may
nevertheless be able to suggest (let us say, for example) the
young man's ardor by a "deep, thrilling" tone of voice. But
given an interpreter who is perfectly responsive, he may vary
his expressive emphasis according to intrinsic qualities of the
piece he is reading. To take a broad example, the interpreter
hardly needs to concern himself during a reading of Oscar
Wilde's *The Importance of Being Earnest,* with Algernon
Moncrieff's body. Algernon's "body" has a very small part to
play in the action, including the love scenes (I do not mean
that the interpreter does not need to think about his own
bodily movements; he may find it more difficult to make
Algernon's body a negative factor than he would to portray
Charles the wrestler). But the interpreter must be more alive
to the expressive possibilities of (let us say) Parkin's body
during a reading of D. H. Lawrence's *Lady Chatterley's Lover,*
in which everywhere "body" is the triumphant foe of "mind."

A clearer example, involving the same expressive-areas,
may be drawn from Thomas Mann's *Death in Venice.* The
famous writer, Aschenbach, has just seen in the physical
beauty of a young boy, Tadzio, playing on the beach before
him, "the same force at work" which he saw in his own attempts to "liberate from the marble mass of language the
slender forms of his art." With this comparison flaming in
his mind, Aschenbach writes a brilliant "little essay" on a
"great and burning question of art and taste." Furthermore,
he writes this essay with Tadzio playing nearby, serving
Aschenbach as "model" of beauty.

The relationship of Aschenbach to Tadzio is a very complicated one: the boy is not for Aschenbach merely a physical
symbol of intellectual beauty. Tadzio is a beautiful boy with
whom the great writer has fallen giddily, and destructively,
in love. The narrator writes of Aschenbach's essay which
"would shortly be the wonder and admiration of the multi-

tude," that "Verily it is well for the world that it sees only the beauty of the completed work and not its origins," and when Aschenbach finishes his essay and leaves the beach, he "felt broken," his "conscience reproached him, as it were after a debauch."

The general movement, then, of the passage—though "mental" and "physical" factors remain interwoven—is from Aschenbach's intellectual apprehension of physical beauty to his internal "physical" participation, to the point of exhaustion, in this apprehension. I once had the pleasure of seeing this movement superbly projected by an oral interpreter. His body, at the beginning of the reading, was tense but quiet and contained, his face alive and extremely expressive (suggesting the "control" of the eager body by the intellectualizing brain; it was once said that the soul shines in the face, and the intense facial expression did most to suggest the vivid thought of Aschenbach). As the reading progressed, the reader's face became ever less expressive, his bodily activity slowly increased. By the end of the passage the reader had practically reversed his original expressive emphasis in the facial-bodily areas. It was a shift which was extremely appropriate to the sense of the passage.

The second of the interpreter's means of expression is that he may more fully develop attitudes which are but implicit in the action.

Take the scene in *Death in Venice* in which Aschenbach falsely thinks he is looking on Tadzio for the last time: "'For the last time, Tadzio,' thought the elder man. 'It was all too brief!' Quite unusually for him, he shaped a farewell with his lips, he actually uttered it, and added, 'May God bless you!'" Given the little description itself, and also our awareness of all that Tadzio has already meant to Aschenbach and of the great deal more that he is going to mean to him, we may say, if we like, that Aschenbach's sorrow, confusion, love, and longing are all *in* the passage. But what happens to the face, the inner "voice" or thoughts, the body of the man at this moment, is very barely described; we know that he shapes a "farewell with his lips," we know that the farewell was spoken, and that is all we are specifically told. The full attitude—the

102

gaze of longing, the brief "frozen" posture, and all the rest of it—must be imagined and created by the interpreter.

Third, the oral interpreter's means of expression may take the form of behavioral synecdoches.

"Behavioral synecdoches" has the sound of jargon, but it is hard to think of a happier description. I mean that the interpreter often suggests a pattern of behavior expressive of a certain attitude by the projection of some aspect of this pattern.

A man in "real life" who is for the moment, let us say, *proudly contemptuous* of some one or some thing, may express that feeling by a slight tossing of his head, a sneer, a laugh, the placing of hand on his hip, and several other more-or-less evident movements. The oral interpreter may project this same attitude by only one or two characteristics of the full pattern (simply by a slight toss of his head, for example).

Sometimes this method is roughly the direct reversal of the interpreter's fuller development of behavior which is only implicit in the piece: a very full written description of behavior may be suggested by only a few details presented orally.

Frequently, however, the situation is more complicated than this: a certain kind of behavior, only implicit in or suggested by the piece, will then be suggested by the oral reader's projection of a few details of that behavior. Put another way, a certain behavior suggested by the writer's own synecdoches is eventually communicated to an audience by other synecdoches expressed by the oral reader.

Let us consider the scene in which the enamored Aschenbach comes close to making a direct physical approach to Tadzio. He is ready to "utter a friendly salutation in French" to the boy, who is walking just ahead of him, unconscious of Aschenbach's presence. But just as he is about to touch Tadzio, Aschenbach "found his heart throbbing unpleasantly fast, while his breath came in such quick pants that he could only have gasped had he tried to speak. He hesitated, sought after self-control," was suddenly "panic-stricken," etc.

Now, implicit in this scene is Aschenbach's complete confusion and loss of control. This is the "total" behavior which the interpreter must project. But, obviously, he cannot simply "go to pieces" before the audience. For one thing, if he does so, his audience will probably just laugh at him; for another, the interpreter, unlike the actor, for reasons which we have already discussed, will not trot across the stage to represent Aschenbach's pursuit of Tadzio.

Yet, the fact remains that in this scene Aschenbach *has* gone to pieces and this must be suggested by the interpreter. It is, with this situation confronting him, that the interpreter will probably rely on behavioral synecdoches. In the best reading of the passage that I have heard, certain aspects of the written description were (rather faintly) preserved in the oral performance: the passage was read rather rapidly, which suggested the unpleasantly fast pounding of Aschenbach's heart; there was a certain breathlessness in performance, which suggested Aschenbach's breathing in "quick pants." But the especially telling gesture came on the reading of the phrase: "He hesitated, sought after self-control . . . ." At this point in his reading, the oral interpreter rapidly licked his lips with the tip of his tongue. The written passage, of course, makes no mention of this; yet it seems to be an unusually appropriate gesture to suggest Aschenbach's agitation. In his search for self-control, we may imagine that Aschenbach becomes for the first time aware of his own state, of how dry his mouth has become, of his whole unpleasant condition. The little nervous licking of lips suggests Aschenbach's whole physical condition, his self-deprecation, his return to self-awareness.

This is, of course, a delicate point: unquestionably, the licking of the lips was only part of a cluster of activities in the oral reading itself, all of which were as necessary to produce conviction as they are ultimately too complex for analysis to tabulate. But, just as certainly, given other proper activity, the half-second movement of the tongue was a superbly summary gesture which was truly the interpreter's "creation." Oral interpreters need not blush at the pettiness of such triumphs; just as a number of little words put together right give us convincing writing, so do a number of little gestures like these, put together right, give us convincing performance.

Whether expressions like these are planned or are simply sensitive responses would seem to be an irrelevant matter. Probably most summary gestures, at least, are a combination of both. In rehearsal, during one reading or another, the interpreter does something which strikes him as somehow especially appropriate and which he then "plans" into his final performance.

You will notice that there is a creative element in the oral interpreter's expression of a text. However, his creativity is — or ought to be — in the service of effects of the text itself. The proper interpreter will not merely respond to his private sense of an attitude, action, or object, apart from the formed perception of it which is represented in the piece.

Such a reader might be, for example, a person whom a ship ride always makes seasick. He would then seek to convey this sense of seasickness in reading the following lines from "Sir Patrick Spens":

Mak hast, mak hast, my mirry men all,
Our guid schip sails the morne.

There is no hint whatever, of course, in the poem that the sea makes anybody ill. Although the reader, as performer, might brilliantly convey the sense of nausea, it would nevertheless be a ludicrously inappropriate reading of the poem.

It is hard to believe that even any of the elocutionists had so false a sense of what it means to interpret a piece, though they are sometimes accused of such humorously misleading responses. At any rate, today, no competent instructor will accept random private impressions as an adequate interpretation of a piece, no matter how skillful the student may be at projecting false impressions.

SUGGESTIONS FOR FURTHER READING

This bibliography is largely limited to some of the books and articles cited in this volume, which may be read with special interest by students of oral interpretation of literature.

Lee Anderson. "How Not to Read Poems – A Dissenting View," *Art and the Craftsman,* ed. Joseph Harned and Neil Goodwin. Carbondale, Ill.: Southern Illinois University Press, 1962. Discussion of values or oral interpretation in teaching poetry by the Director of Yale Series of Recorded Poets.

Wallace Bacon and Robert Breen. *Literature as Experience.* New York: McGraw-Hill Book Co., 1959. Experiential theory of oral interpretation. Good bibliography of materials relevant to oral interpretation drawn from psychology and literary criticism.

Monroe Beardsley, Robert Daniel, and Glenn Leggett. *Theme and Form.* Englewood Cliffs, N.J.: Prentice-Hall, Inc., 1956. An anthology of literary selections organized around major themes. Includes brief, efficient essays on structure of literature and its various modes.

Henri Bergson. *The Creative Mind,* trans. Mabelle L. Andison. New York: Philosophical Library, Inc., 1946. Suggests values in distinguishing concrete knowledge of metaphysics and art from abstract knowledge of science.

R. P. Blackmur. *Language as Gesture.* New York: Harcourt, Brace & Company, 1952. Close analysis, through the study of specific poets, of the art of poetry as a language of gesture.

Cleanth Brooks. *The Well Wrought Urn.* New York: Harcourt, Brace & Company, 1947. Essays on specific poems emphasizing the organic relations of art and meaning in poetry and emphasizing poetry as dramatic discourse.

Cleanth Brooks and Robert Penn Warren, eds. *Understanding Fiction.* New York: F. S. Crofts & Company, 1943. An anthology of stories which includes many suggestions for reliable approaches to the analysis of fiction.

Kenneth Burke. *The Philosophy of Literary Form.* Rev. ed. New York: Vintage Books, Inc., 1957. Provocative theory of poetry as symbolic action, and other essays in rhetoric and poetic.

Kenneth Burke. *A Rhetoric of Motives.* New York: Prentice-Hall, Inc., 1950. An elaborate theory of persuasion as identification, including incidental illustrations of poetry as symbolic action.

John Ciardi, ed. *Mid-Century American Poets* (containing especially Richard Wilbur, "The Genie in the Bottle"). New York: Twayne Publishers, 1950. Selections of poems from fifteen recent American poets. Includes essays by the poets on their attitudes toward the writing and oral reading of verse, and other relevant matters.

R. S. Crane, ed. *Critics and Criticism* (containing especially Elder Olson, "An Outline of Poetic Theory"). Chicago: University of Chicago Press, 1952. A large showcase of neo-Aristotelian theory of poetry, and related subjects.

Samuel Silas Curry. *Imagination and Dramatic Instinct.* Boston: School of Expression, 1896. A study of vocal expression as revelation of the speaker's processes of thinking and feeling.

David Daiches. "The New Criticism: Some Qualifications," *College English,* XI (1950), 242-250. Suggests some strictures against leading ideas of modern criticism and emphasizes values to literary students of oral reading.

Donald Hargis. "Interpretation as Oral Communication," *Central States Speech Journal,* XI (1960), 168-173. Reviews briefly, with critical reservations, emphases in modern oral interpretation theory and includes selective bibliography of this theory.

Donald Hargis. "What Is Oral Interpretation?" *Western Speech,* XVI (1952), 175-180. Emphasizes importance of vocal and delivery factors in oral interpretation.

S. I. Hayakawa. *Language in Thought and Action.* New York: Harcourt, Brace & Company, 1949. Summarizes basic principles of general semantics in relation to speech and literature.

George Hemphill, ed. *Discussions of Poetry: Rhythm and*

Sound (containing especially Seymour Chatman, "Robert Frost's 'Mowing': An Inquiry into Poetic Structure," and Thomas Jefferson, from "Thoughts on English Prosody"). Boston: D. C. Heath & Company, 1961. Anthology of important articles on prosody from sixteenth century to the present.

Susanne K. Langer. *Philosophy in a New Key.* Cambridge: Harvard University Press, 1942. Essay in aesthetic theory emphasizing possibilities for doctrines of art as a form of knowledge, or cognitive discourse.

Charles Laughton. "Read It Out Loud," *This Week,* November 19, 1950. Advice on the pleasures of reading literature aloud from a professional reader.

Charlotte Lee. *Oral Interpretation.* Boston: Houghton Mifflin Co., 1959. Principles of reading aloud, including brief history of oral interpretation theory.

Norman F. MacLean. "An Analysis of a Lyric Poem," *The University Review,* VIII (1942), 202-209. Shows semantic function of rime in close "neo-Aristotelian" analysis of one of Wordsworth's poems.

John Crowe Ransom. *The World's Body.* New York: Charles Scribner's Sons, 1938. Poetry presented as man's most complete form of knowledge.

George F. Reynolds. "Oral Interpretation as Graduate Work in English," *College English,* XI (1950), 204-210. Stresses importance of oral interpretation in graduate study.

I. A. Richards. *Practical Criticism.* New York: Harcourt, Brace & Company, 1950. Penetrating analysis of British literary students' reactions to specific poems.

I. A. Richards. *Principles of Literary Criticism.* New York: Harcourt, Brace & Company, 1925. A seminal work of modern literary theory.

Gerald Sanders. *A Poetry Primer.* New York: Farrar, Straus and Cudahy, Inc., 1935. On the nature and forms of poetry.

Thomas A. Sebeok, ed. *Style in Language* (containing especially Benjamin Hrushovski, "On Free Rhythms in Modern Poetry" and W. K. Wimsatt and Monroe Beardsley, "The Concept of Meter: an Exercise in Abstraction" [abstract]). New York: John Wiley & Sons, Inc., 1960. A large collection of articles showing something of the approach of modern linguists, psychologists, and other behavioral scientists toward various aspects of language. A long section of modern theories of metrical and prosodic analysis.

R. W. Stallman, ed. *Critiques and Essays in Criticism,* 1920-1948 (containing especially Kenneth Burke, "Lexicon Rhetoricae," D. G. James, "I. A. Richards," and Eliseo Vivas, "The Objective Correlative of T. S. Eliot"). New York: The Ronald Press Company, 1949. Anthology of essays in modern literary criticism. Good bibliography of modern criticism.

Mona Van Duyn. "What's Happening to Prose?" *College English,* XVI (1954), 18-24. An account of developments in modern writing and comment on reading habits of modern audience of serious literature.

William Van O'Connor. "A Short View of the New Criticism," *College English,* XI (1949), 63-71. Sympathetic account of leading ideas of much modern criticism.

René Wellek and Austin Warren. *Theory of Literature.* New York: Harcourt, Brace & Company, 1956. Thorough description of the nature and function of literature, and of literary scholarship. Copious and valuable notes and bibliography in modern literary scholarship.

Ray B. West, Jr., ed. *Essays in Modern Literary Criticism* (containing especially Samuel Taylor Coleridge, from "Biographia Literaria, XIV," and John Crowe Ransom, "Criticism as Pure Speculation"). New York: Rinehart & Company, Inc., 1952. Anthology of essays in modern literary criticism. Good bibliography of twentieth-century criticism.

Alfred North Whitehead. *The Aims of Education.* New York: The Macmillan Company, 1929. Attitudes of a significant modern philosopher toward education.

Richard Wilbur. "Commentary," Symposium on Richard Wilbur, *Berkeley Review 3,* (1958), 47-51. Essay by an excellent modern poet on the formal and structural achievements inherent in good poetry.

W. K. Wimsatt and Monroe Beardsley. "The Concept of Meter," *PMLA,* LXXIV (1959), 585-598. A "traditionalist" account of meter, with some strictures against certain emphases in theory of prosodic analysis by structural linguists.

Yvor Winters. *In Defense of Reason.* Denver: Alan Swallow, 1947. Essays in literary criticism arguing, interestingly if somewhat dogmatically, for the importance of rational ordering of moral content in poetry.

Judith Wray. "Theories and Methods of Representative Contemporary Poets as Readers of Their Own Poetry" (Ph. D. abstract), *Speech Monographs,* XXIX, No. 2 (1962), 114-115. Discussion of attitudes toward oral reading taken by numerous contemporary poets.

INDEX

Acting, 14
  oral interpretation related to,
    79-82
Actions, as expressible elements in
  a text, 97
Aesthetic distance, 80-81, 87-88
"An Essay on Criticism," 42-43
Analysis, of poem as preparation
  for performance, 15-17
  See also Dramatic analysis of
    literature
Anderson, Lee, 55-56
Appreciation, of literature, 19-21,
  28-29
Art, oral interpretation as, 89
"Ash Wednesday," 21
Attitude
  defined, 94
  expressible element in text, 93-94
  expression of properties of objects
    related to, 96-97.
  implicit, developed by interpreter,
    102-103
  performance based on, 12-17
  relationship to situation
    in literature, 61-65
  unifying principle of a poem,
    11-12
  See also Emotion *and* Semantic
    structure
Attitudinal approach. *See* Experiential approach
Audience
  consideration of, in choice of
    material, 76-78
  expectations of, 83
  interpreter as member of au-
    thor's, 85-86
  motivation to reader, 17
  shared literary experience with-
    in, 17-18

Auditory imagination, in realization of a poem's sound-structure, 44
Auditory metaphor, suggestion of
  properties by, 95-96
Author, identification of interpreter
  with, 82-83
  See also Poets

Baldwin, Charles S., 35
Beardsley, Monroe C., 37-40, 41, 46,
  47, 49
Behavioral synecdoches, means of
  expression by interpreter,
  103-104
Benét, Stephen V., 56, 57
Bergson, Henri, 16-17
Blackmur, R. P., 12, 18, 60, 99
Bodily movement
  in oral interpretation, 88
  means of expressing a text,
    100-104
Brooks, Cleanth, 11-12, 40-41, 69
Burke, Kenneth, 12, 18, 31, 63
Burns, Robert, 45

Carnap, Rudolph, 12
Chatman, Seymour, 42-43, 50-51
Ciardi, John, 58
Classroom, oral reading in, 76
  See also Instructor *and* Student
Coleridge, Samuel T., 75
Communication
  oral interpretation as art of,
    79-91
  means of interpreter for, 78
  literature as, 77-78
Complexity, of literature, 20-21
Crane, Hart, 19

113